C000255614

the
last
courtesan

writing my mother's memoir

manish
gaekwad

HarperCollins *Publishers* India

First published in India by HarperCollins *Publishers* 2023
4th Floor, Tower A, Building No 10, DLF Cyber City,
DLF Phase II, Gurugram, Haryana – 122002
www.harpercollins.co.in

2 4 6 8 10 9 7 5 3 1

Copyright © Manish Gaekwad 2023

P-ISBN: 978-93-5699-312-9
E-ISBN: 978-93-5699-306-8

The views and opinions expressed in this book are the author's own
and the facts are as reported by him, and the publishers are not in
any way liable for the same.

Manish Gaekwad asserts the moral right
to be identified as the author of this work.

Some names have been changed for legal reasons.

All rights reserved. No part of this publication may be reproduced,
stored in a retrieval system, or transmitted, in any form or by any means,
electronic, mechanical, photocopying, recording or otherwise,
without the prior permission of the publishers.

Typeset in 11.5/15.2 Adobe Garamond at
Manipal Technologies Limited, Manipal

Printed and bound at
Replika Press Pvt. Ltd.

This book is produced from independently certified FSC® paper to ensure
responsible forest management.

To my mother, Rekha Devi, who used to sing '*Maa mujhe apne aanchal mein chhupa le/ Galey se lagaa le/ Ke aur mera koi nahi*' as a lullaby to me. She could see my future repeat her past, and melodiously hummed for our hearts to love.

Introduction

I HAVE ENTERTAINED THE THOUGHT OF KILLING MY MOTHER. MULTIPLE methods have shimmy-shimmied on the dance floor of my neon-lit mind. As we sway under the pink and purple lights, I stylishly club her head with a blunt utensil from her filthy kitchen – in particular, that hideous, black-bottomed aluminium begging bowl in which she cooks her fragrant, small-grain, gulab swaroop rice. Or I choke her gutka-scented breath with a musty white bolster that's shining like a strange, fluorescent weapon in one dark corner of her bed, as if it is a discarded artefact of an unrecorded era no one wants to return to. I chuckle when such visions tickle my thalamus. A tingling sensation jerks through my body, in the same manner as, pardon me, a steaming log of stool passes through my anus. I know I sound wholly inappropriate, so I'll try sober.

I often think of my mother's death for a great opening sentence like Camus' in *The Stranger*: Mother died today. Or maybe yesterday, I don't know.

A few years ago, my friend Pravesh and I were walking behind the Versova dargah, which also houses a poorly maintained cemetery. My first book was going to be published soon. You should write about your mother next, he said. I took a long sigh, smiled, feeling the cool air of the tall coconut trees from the cemetery reach us like a cue, and agreed with him, saying I only know the beginning. I don't have an end. And just like that, a coconut should have fallen at that moment and been my end for thinking aloud.

My mother's death, I have mulled for many years, would be the only way for me to write about her and best Camus. It has little to do with my quest for an immortal line, and more with finding a befitting end to her story. Her story reads well, I am aware of that; so engagingly well, in fact, that I worry from the very beginning, because I know the end before she gets there. The end is so ordinary, dull, forgotten and unsaleable that death alone can revitalize it with a scandal: an unheard, extraordinary tale of survival.

Of course, I don't want to kill her, although a jail just might be the perfect place for writing. I mean the forcible sex, whose unjust rewards I might resentfully enjoy more for the heck of gathering material for another book, along with feeling a kinship with Wilde.

I would want her to die to save her the embarrassment of finding out the unkind things I am going to be revealing about her. Or not die, and survive this too. As long as she does not learn how to read in English, I am safe. She did, however, ask me, on the release of my first novel: Why is it not *dubbed* in Hindi? She is cute like that. Simple people are. Cute and regrettable. She should get selective amnesia when my version of her story raises a stink. I already see her reaction: Maine aisa kab kaha tha? When did I say such a thing?

When I tell her my earliest memory of her involved a drunkard she was fighting with, and in which one of her fingers was chopped off, she says that never happened. Who will believe her if I don't?

But you told me that when I was a child.

Tu aur tera dimaag; marwa ke rahega hum sab ko. You and your imagination will get us killed.

I beg to differ. Aphantasia might.

I saw it with my own eyes. A young servant girl was cradling me in her arms in the corridor, near the landing of the wooden staircase. You and another woman, one dressed in a black saree, indistinguishable from the other in grey, were pulling and pushing a tall man who was flashing a brilliant silver knife. I was watching helplessly. Listening to your screams, I was fidgeting and crying. I was stretching my hand to reach you as if I could help. That man sliced off your finger. There was blood on the dance floor.

Purani film hogi koi. It must be a scene from a black-and-white film, mother says.

I remember it vividly. Show me your hands.

She holds out her hands.

See, this finger!

I point to the ring finger on her left hand. It is short, wrinkled and stubby.

Haan, yeh toh aise hi lag gaya tha chhuri se kitchen mein. Yes, a knife had nicked this in the kitchen.

She laughs, trying to appear enigmatic about her scars. She is definitely holding back the horrors of the past. She mentions Meena Kumari. Her little finger was also severed in an accident. She used to always keep her hand wrapped in her dupatta or pallu. She never showed it on-screen.

Woh yun ek haath se action karti thi '*Chalte chalte*' mein. She used her right hand emotively in the song '*Chalte chalte*'.

Mother imitates Meena Kumari's mudras with ease.

My mother thinks of herself as a tragedienne like the actress – unwanted and unloved. The pitiable story of any tawaif's life, actually. Many become obsessed with their unending gham, misery, retracing into a flashback. Mother didn't do it in the beginning, but, as she began to fade in the kotha, alone and aloof, she became Meena Kumari. The drinking, the loneliness, the sad songs and the constant reference to dard, pain – in her case, bloating, gas and sinus allergies became her loyal patrons, visiting her more often than common sense.

I realize that she is going to fudge. A lot. Not an easy subject, but not as clever as she thinks she is. I have heard her story in bits and pieces over the years. I have seen things to ratiocinate her grainy memory of the past. In the twenty-odd years I stayed away from her, not by guilt of association, and for which I feel a pressing urgency to absolve myself first, but to charter my own destiny, I have understood her more intimately than I would have had I not detached myself from the care of her motherly aanchal. 'Chanda ko dhoondne sabhi taare nikal gaye', she used to sing me the depressing lullaby, fanning my head with her pallu, weeping and ruining my sleep. Why is she crying, I wondered, but dared not ask.

Like her, I too have lived alone and aloof for most of my life. I grew up in kothas and in boarding schools, drifted as an adolescent, and stepped out of her overbearing shadow as soon as I completed college. We don't share a typical mother-son relationship, there is no love lost, but there is no spectacle either. We meet like strangers, trying to read the other as politely as possible, treading softly, observing and engaging with humour. There is a definite wall between us. We are looking for a crack to let the neon light pass and illuminate both sides. She never weighs what she wants to say. I measure its worth. She never ever fully realized till now that, one day, she will have to recount her story for a cheap paperback, or so she thinks of my idea to write about her life. Kaun padhega? Who is going to read it? she asks. Kya zaroorat hai purani baatein ukhaadna? What's the point of raking up the past? She fears the samaaj, society.

She knows I write for a living, but she would have preferred a more stable career for me. Why did you choose such a hard life?

She worries it is a job fraught with rejection and despair. Jaise *Pyaasa* mein Guru Dutt. Like Guru Dutt in *Pyaasa*, she says. Kaun samjhega teri yeh shayari-wairi, yeh kahani-wahani, teri yeh wordings? Who will appreciate your poems, stories, your words? Mujhe toh bahut pehle pataa chal gaya tha tu doctor nahi bann sakta; khoon dekh ke ghabra jaata hai. Bank mein lag jaata. Zindagi aaram se kat jaati. I knew you would not become a doctor when I saw how blood made you nauseous. You could have worked in a bank, at least. You would have had a comfortable life.

Oh, comfort – that elusive creature of habit.

If your story sells, we will both have a comfortable life, I assure her. Tell me like it is.

Is she mentally preparing for a pulpy story like the Hindi crime novels of Ved Prakash, Gulshan Nanda, Om Prakash, Aadil Rashid and Surender Mohan Pathak, which she used to read in the kotha? I surely am. This is her chance to set the record straight. The music will be hers to play. I will scratch beneath the surface like an intrepid deejay remixing '*Chanda ko dhoondne sabhi taare nikal gaye*'. All the stars will twinkle to look for the missing moon in the disco-blue sky.

Poona

I DO NOT KNOW WHEN I WAS BORN. EVEN MY PARENTS WOULD NOT KNOW if you asked them. But they have been dead a long time. I never got a chance to ask them.

My being born was not an event. I was born at night, in a ramshackle hut on the outskirts of Poona. The tin hut was situated on a barren, dusty stretch on the side of a highway. On the other side were green fields. Fields as fertile as dreams we had never seen. In our homes, children are born like litter – one right after another. And, in the cold night, if one dies of neglect, there is no time to grieve.

I once heard from my neighbours that my deranged father, Tadiya, wanted to drown me in a pond when I was born. He was fed up of siring girls. I was told that he grabbed me and walked out to fling me out somewhere, but someone persuaded him to calm down. A drunken man's alibi will always be that he was not in his senses. Everyone called him Tadiya because he drank too

1

much taadi, toddy. Tadiya sounded like a cuss word. Something
one would say to shoo away an unwelcome person. Aye, tadiya!
He was a scraggy, lean man who always tilted to one side as he
tried to stand up straight. Maybe he was trying to leap to the
other side as fast as he could. He worked as a watchman in a
motor company at night and slept all day. That is the main reason
why he was always leaning towards eternal rest. I do not know
his real first name. I never asked him. Since everyone called him
Tadiya and he did not mind it, so did mother. The elder sisters
also secretly called him Tadiya when he was not around. It never
occurred to me that he would have any other name, as this one
fitted the description of a foul-smelling, unkempt and garrulous
man. I heard his surname was Tamaichikar during panchayat
meetings when some elderly man spoke about our samaj and our
responsibilities. Tadiya was from the Kanjarbhat community, a
nomadic tribe from Rajasthan. His eyes were always watery and
red. He had a thick moustache suited to a noble and judicious
sarpanch. Except that he always made the worst decisions. Like
trying to kill me.

My mother, Gulshan Devi, was always dressed in a flowy, long
black skirt and a three-quarter-sleeved blouse with a mirrored flap
in the front. The mirror was often broken. We checked our faces
in the mirror that had more cracks than our sunburnt faces. She
draped an odhni covering her head and drew a big red tika on her
forehead with some coloured powder. That was her only make-
up. She wore a silver hansli necklace, glass bangles and thick tode
anklets, probably the only pieces of jewellery she had. She never
took them off, perhaps fearing that they would get stolen. Her body
was the only safe place to keep them. She used to sew money inside
the hem of her ghagra, where she had made secret pockets. She was
a chalta-phirta bank, jaise aaj kal ka ATM. She had many tattoos on
her arms, some green dots on the sides of her eyes, and under her

chin and neck. With a mouth turned downwards and hazy brown eyes, she did not seem friendly at all. She belonged to the Gujjar tribe, people who work as caretakers of livestock and in fields as labourers. Whenever she had to speak of us to someone, she used to say, 'Sab apne naseeb se paida hote hain.' One is born of their own destiny. Surviving the night of the birth was not guaranteed. She had the look of surrender on her face that only comes to those who accept loss in life without the fear of having ever owned anything.

My mother worked in the fields for some landowner. She grew hara bhara, chickpea; seng, peanut; bajra, pearl millet; jowar, sorghum; and tamatar, tomato. At times, she washed dishes at someone's wedding for leftover food. She invested her earnings in cows and goats.

Gullo, as we began to call her when we grew up, never sang a lullaby. She had no time to waste. She did not even sing in the fields. Her head was only clouded with thoughts of feeding and providing for her family. She could not let go of her husband because she was a good person, who liked tending to helpless beings, like a cow she raised. She must have thought of Tadiya as a helpless animal. What was she to do of a man like that? Maybe she felt like a defective baby-producing machine, whose function was to ultimately give him a male child and prove her own worth as a woman. Till then, she suffered in silence. When I think of her now, I think it affected us, how we grew up to think our main purpose was to produce babies, rear them and keep the family together.

I think we nine sisters also grew up understanding the importance of a man in the house. A male child was anticipated, and expected of her. The nine of us were on display as failed attempts. We may have felt unwanted or unloved, but we did not know any better as we did not have the time to think and seek love and affection from our parents. We simply crowded in a corner of the room. We had no voice. We were mute to our existence.

The sound of an orange flame crackling under a black pot filled with cloudy rice water was music to us in the evening after we returned from the pastures. I must have been five when I began herding goats along with my sisters.

There were five sisters before me – Ranjana, Anjana, Babbo, Shehzaadi and Gora. Three survived. Ranjana and Anjana died soon after birth. I heard that one of them died of a high fever and a snake bit the other. Mother was working in a field, where she had made a hammock out of a cloth between two trees, and put the infant girl to sleep. A snake slid in and bit the girl. Three more were born after me – Rohini, Shanna and Laccha. Then we had a brother in the end, Dasrath. Nine girls for a boy. You can say we were like the nine manifestations of Durga devi, but all in vain for a male child named after the king Dasharatha in the Ramayana: The man who could move in ten directions. But right now, that wasteful brother of mine is lying immobile in a shanty in Poona. He is bloating in no particular direction, bas phail raha hai.

I am the sixth-born. The fierce one. The Durga who slayed the buffalo demon Mahishasura, as written in the Puranas. When Tadiya wanted to drown me, he could not. I grew up with the rumour that I had defeated death. It did not make me haughty; it made me go quiet. Did I really have such power? I spent my childhood looking for a sign, but I did not find any evidence of it. I wandered in the fields, on the moor, in the streets. I was lost. I do not know if I was looking for anything to substantiate what living means.

Another instance of me defying death comes to my mind now. I was walking with my drunken father through a jungle. We were returning from another village, where we had gone to meet a relative. It was very late in the night. A wispy figure was walking ahead of us.

Do you know the way to Pimpri? My father asked the person ahead of us.

Yes, he said. Follow me.

The man ahead did not turn to look at us. My father had no sense of direction. He stumbled and followed the shadowy figure. We reached a crossroads. My father walked towards the strange black apparition.

Father, I said, we have to go in this other direction. That road leads to a khaai, a ditch.

The shadow was misleading us. Suddenly, we heard hurried footsteps ahead. As if the shadow was running. It disappeared into the night like a ghost. My father came to his senses. He asked me to turn my face away. He walked ahead and urinated in the mud. He then made four mud balls of his urine and flung one in each direction. He did this to ward off evil, to chase death away. He believed the shadow was Death leading us to the ditch. My alertness saved us. After that incident, my father did not begrudge my existence. I had saved his life too. He did not do anything special to make me feel better. He just treated me like he did the other sisters, indifferent to us growing up as cats or wolves in a litter. That incident might be the first time I became curious about the unknown.

I began venturing out alone. A song that I remember hearing as a child was 'O Phirkiwali. Tu kal phir aana'. I do not know where I had heard it, but I liked it a lot. I am guessing it was playing on a radio in some shop. I liked following tunes. I would reach the source from where it was coming, like a shop or a house, and wait outside and listen attentively. These songs would dance in my heart like waves of happiness. I felt good, but stood still, looking lost, and often forgetting that I was supposed to be tending goats. My behaviour often got me into trouble, as I would wander far away with the cattle.

Who is a phirkiwali? I asked Gullo once. She said it must be to some boogeywoman. She had other important business to attend to than indulge me.

Where did you meet this phirkiwali? Gullo shot back.

I have not, I said, earning her trust. Singing and dancing was not commonplace in our hut. Where was the room to dance?

I sang the melody in the pastures, herding the goats with a stick that I waved in the air like a wand to ward off evil in our way: *O Phirkiwali, tu kal phir aana.* I had memorized only the first line of the lyrics. I whistled the rest of the melody. *La-la-lala-lala.*

I had a pet goat, a fluffy white kid called Neelkamal. I loved her so much. We talked and walked miles together. She was also chatty. She was a puny goat with stubby horns. Once, when she was older, she gave birth to a kid. It fell out of her stomach in a jelly sack. That is how I thought babies fell out. That is how I was going to drop a baby some day, I thought, as I looked on in horror. It will just fall out of me into the world. And then? I did not know how to think further. I could not. My thought was limited by our poverty. It would have been indulgent to think beyond our little hut in the world where we girls were like cattle, grazing and being prepared to produce like an animal.

Gullo was also a dai, a midwife. She and another dai, Chavvani, helped a lot of women with childcare. Gullo also had a cow named Laali. It was because of Laali that she was able to raise so many daughters. Laali was a greater source of milk than Gullo. She was always pregnant and did not have the time to breastfeed her own infants. Laali's teats were squeezed into our mouths. Gullo was as ancient as time itself; she raised children and animals with an instinct or a wisdom that seemed to come from within her. She did not have to consult anyone to break our tonsil stones or fix a broken bone. Her home-made potions and ointments from herbs and spices would cure us of common ailments.

Once, while playing kho-kho, a girl pushed me. I knocked my head on a metal pillar. My skin tore. A long gash spilt blood from my forehead. Gullo used some herbal paste made of imli ka chhal, tamarind skin, and wrapped it in resham, silk. She bandaged it to my head. After it healed, there was a nishaan, scar. Some kids teased me that I had a third eye. I turned quiet. Gullo told me the eye was a good mark; it was a sign of my naseeb, which we carry like a lifelong burden in our heart. Tu apna naseeb khud hi banaegi. You will make your own destiny.

Gullo would make phepsi, a concoction of milk with gur, jaggery. It was a sweet dish she made only on festive occasions. She did not fuss over us or show any preferential treatment to the girls. She did that only when Dasrath was born. After nine unsuccessful attempts, she had decided this was going to be her last chance. She, too, perhaps wanted to put her womb up for retirement. How much more could she produce? She was like a cow to Tadiya.

Tadiya was not the most faithful of men. He slept with her younger sister, Shalu, and sired another child. Shalu used to come to our house to help Gullo during her pregnancy. Tadiya was a drunkard. Shalu was jawaan, young. Lafda ho gaya. There was an affair. When Shalu had a son, Gullo was more elated than them. She wanted to keep the baby. But our panchayat decided the baby must be sent away to an orphanage and Shalu must be married to a decent suitor. All this happened before I was born. I would meet the boy much later in life. His name was Ashok.

Dasrath's birth was a cause for celebration. We sisters could see it in Gullo's eyes that sparkled. She breastfed him. She played with him, gave him regular massages to strengthen his bones and made him eat more food than he could, to make him walk as quickly as he could. It did not make us jealous, but instead our eyes glazed over when we saw her fussing over her son. Maybe he was special. It is what we saw and experienced. It made us sisters do exactly as our mother, treat the little boy like a hero who would grow up to look after us, protect us and make a better male figure than our indifferent father.

Many years later, a cow killed Tadiya. He sat down to collect milk from one of Laali's daughters. She kicked him in the chest. He could not breathe. He requested Gullo to fetch him alcohol. She sold the milk for taadi. He drank the alcohol, felt relieved and died. Gullo adjusted her odhni in deference and said, Uske naseeb mein yehi tha. This was in his destiny.

Once, my elder sister, Shehzaadi, was going out with some of her friends. I followed her. She kept asking me to return home, but I did not listen to her. We reached the Khadki military cantonment, or maybe it was Dapodi. The jawans used to watch films inside a big hall room with open windows. My sisters would climb a wall to watch from the outside.

This is how I saw the film *Khandaan*. It had a beautiful song, '*Tumhi meri mandir*'. At that time, I did not know who had sung it. I was engrossed in watching the lovely heroine take care of a paralysed husband. She was singing a lorie to put him to sleep. That is how I knew a lorie should sound. A lorie that our mother did not sing to us in bed, or to her passed-out drunkard husband, Tadiya.

I began following my sister quite often to watch from the fenced wall. I did not yet know her name then, but Meena Kumari felt the most real to me. In *Phool Aur Patthar*, a man molests her. I screamed, Madarchod! Maaro na usko. Motherfucker, somebody thrash him. I had heard Hindi-speaking people use the cuss word. I blurted it out in the heat of the moment.

Aye, sssh, Babbo, my other sister said. This is a film.

What is that? I asked.

What we are seeing is not real, she said.

I did not ask her any questions. I did not want to miss anything. It is only after I came to Calcutta later that I saw a screen up close and understood. Seeing Meena Kumari on screen always made me cry as if she was my badi didi. If she cried, I cried. And she cried a lot.

I could relate to her. She was expressive and always played characters of real women. I learnt a lot just by watching her talk, move, smile. She had a poise, a femininity that was altogether her own. Every time I saw her, I thought all those hardships she faced were the same as mine. Her sadness resonated with me.

I do not remember many things about my childhood other than my sisters braiding my hair and making me carry gunny bags of rice and wheat to load on to a train for some money. I am not even sure if I got any of that money for a snack. We used to make gotey most times. Cow-dung cakes for the fireplace.

I liked looking for twigs and branches for the mitti ka chulha at home. The fire in the chulha was a beast that snapped the wood like brittle bones – its hunger was insatiable. I fed the fire just to hear the crackling sounds and the quiet hum it made. It was a chore that made me jump and laugh if the flames rose high. It was a kind of cheap entertainment for me to play with the fire. 'Duur hat,' Gullo used to say, using a bhoogli, a hollow iron rod to blow air into the chulha to make orange and blue flames dance around the pots. Our hut roared all day with activity and slept peacefully when the sun went down. We did not have electricity and water or oil for lamps, so it was only the fire from the chulha that lit our faces in the dark, by which time we sat around its silent glow, eating our meals, gossiping and making our beds to sleep on.

There used to be a pond where we used to bathe. Since we did not have a change of clothes, we used to wash the ghagra-cholis we were wearing and wait for them to dry in the sun as we sat naked in the tall grasses, chatting and laughing.

We used to sneak into fields to steal tomatoes, onions and chillies to flavour our rice broth. We would steal the jowar ka baal and roast it on a flame for a crunchy snack. Some days, we had to sleep hungry on half a jowar roti. Gullo would pat one giant roti on the tawa and after it was baked, would break it into four equal halves and give us one portion each. Since we could not afford meat she would get goat blood from a butcher and make a pudding. She would boil it on high flame, adding onion, tomatoes, ginger, garlic and spices till it turned thick like jelly. We did not enjoy it much, but we ate it because hunger has no taste. Bhookha kya nahi khaata! The hungry cannot be picky.

One day, I heard a new song. The melody seduced me. I do not remember it now. It was like a pungi serenading a snake. I followed the sound grow louder and louder till I reached the gate of a glass-manufacturing factory. A man spotted me hanging outside the canteen. He said he would pay me ek pai, one paisa, to wash the dirty dishes.

Can you do it? he asked.

Yes, I said.

I secretly went to the factory, where I washed dishes to earn some money. I would not let my sisters find out. It was the hunger of my heart, my soul, that began to nourish my stomach. I used the money to buy a lime pickle I loved so much that I saw in the canteen. A big ball of sun shining in a glass jar. I could eat the sun. I could put it whole in my mouth and swallow the sky. But it was so sour that I nibbled on it all day, eating the sun bit by bit till dusk, sometimes comparing it with the one in the sky that was fading away, by holding it upwards and eclipsing the star.

The glass-bottle-making factory had a garden where I went to pluck flowers. My sisters used to tell me to get the mehndi ke phool. They used to rub the flower in their palms to get an orange tint like on a bride's hands. Then they would compare it with each other to see who had got the brightest hue. It was a sign that the lucky girl would get married first. Since I brought the flowers that had already stained my fingers, I did not much care to play the silly game.

I used to go to the garden on the way to the pond and would sometimes ask the watchman to give me a rose. When he did not, I would pluck one anyway and drop it in the earthen pot I was carrying. I would fill the pot with water and, by the time I reached home, the water would be scented. Drinking it later in the night gave me the satisfaction of eating a rose without chewing on its petals. That feeling always compensated for having little or no food to eat. Scented water satiated my soul.

When I was nine or ten, my parents got me married to a young man. My sisters gossiped that my dead grandmother owed the man's family some money. My mother could not repay it, so she gave me away. I do not know the truth. In those days, there was no proof on paper about loans. My parents were too poor to refute their claim. Did Gullo forsake me? Did she sell me? Was I less dear to her?

I do not know why I was chosen to be given away as a bride. Maybe the groom's family chose me from the litter. Two older sisters, Babbo and Shehzaadi, had been married by the time this happened. But it was not my turn yet.

I have very little recollection of that day, but it must have been a bad day. It should be – if a girl child is being traded off as a bride. I cried a lot and my mother kept crying back, offering no solace. She pushed me towards the groom, Ramlal. She gave me a small bottle of lemon pickle as a parting gift.

Since I was a kanya, a child bride, there was no ceremony. Some elders had gathered in the hut. I was dressed in a sasti si, inexpensive, green silk saree and was seated next to the man. I had no jewellery on me. There were no flowers to colour my palms. No special meal was cooked in the house. No one sang a song. It felt like something ominous was taking place. It was unlike the weddings I had seen of my elder sisters, where everyone was happy. Here, the air was heavy with silence. It felt more like we had gathered to mourn a dead person. Someone from the bustee chanted the mantras to solemnize the marriage. Even those chants felt like a prayer for the peaceful migration of the soul. Where was I being sent away? I had no clue. Frightened, but quiet, I knew that resisting it could harm my family and me.

Ramlal was not a nice man. I realized that when I was left alone with him in a room. He forced himself on me. It was just like in the movie with Meena Kumari. The only difference was that there was a hero in the movie to save her. Here, I was on my own. No one would come to my rescue. It was a situation with the full sanction of two families. I tried resisting him without screaming. My anger and rage were internal. He overpowered me. I was bleeding and crying, beating my hands and legs to escape his weight on top of me. He put a hand to my mouth. I did not bite it. I did not want to be beaten up while he was forcing himself on me. It could have been worse. I was brutalized in a way that I have tried to erase it completely from my memory, as if it never happened. But the truth is so horrible that even recollecting it makes me recoil in horror. I did not understand that I had been violated. We did not know what a good touch or a bad touch was. We did not know that this was what men wanted from girls. We did not know that there was another way of asking for it. If we were going to be married, our husband had a right to our body without asking for our permission. I had not even grown up as an adult to grant or deny that permission. All I knew was that I was now married to this man and I would have to do as he said. He owned me. I had no say. For a girl who seldom opened her mouth, how was I going to raise my voice? I did not know how to speak for myself. I did not know my rights. I had never seen such things in my house. There were no men to fight and learn from. We were quiet, obedient girls being raised by our resilient mother. We were going to be like her.

Someone took Ramlal and me to a photo studio the next day. I was wearing the same saree from the wedding night.

Yeh dulhan hai? the photographer asked Ramlal. Is she the bride?

Ramlal nodded.

Iske gehne nahi hai? Does she not have jewellery?

Ramlal shook his head.

The photographer arranged for some fake jewellery. A gold necklace was clumsily placed on my chest where it sat askew. I was asked to wear some green bangles. With no finger rings, toe rings, anklets, nose pin or earrings, the bridal look felt incomplete. I did not have an odhni on my head like a coy bride. I looked blankly into the camera when the photographer asked us to smile. I still have that photograph as a reminder that by then I had forgotten how to smile. My childhood had been snatched from me. How could I smile?

Mailani

After two days, we travelled to a small town called Mailani in Uttar Pradesh. Tadiya had accompanied us on the journey by train. It was the first time I was travelling in a train. All I remember is looking out of the window. I wondered when it would stop so that I could get down and eat something. I was hungry. I did not want to finish the bottle of lemon pickle I was carrying. I wanted to save some for my new home. My father was sleeping. I did not want to wake him up and ask for food.

I did not respect my father at all. I loved my mother very much. I had become quiet and resilient like her. Ramlal was like my father from day one. Asserting his power. Or maybe he was doing as was expected of him. I mean, he was still a young man who had a long way to go before he could earn any respect. He was not a man to talk to. For now, he was just my husband, a brute male force I was no match for. How could I tell him my feelings? What feelings did I have for him? I did not even know him. This strange, new man whom I was supposed to listen to and obey for the rest of my life. I was not trained to speak back if he said something. Just do as he says, I was told by my mother.

My father left soon after we got to a house in Mailani. We stayed there for a few days. I do not remember now whose house it was. Then Ramlal took me to Agra. His house was in the Rui Ki Mandi area of Shahganj. A door opened into a courtyard with rooms on either side. There was a water tap on one side, a khaat on another. It was much nicer than my mother's hut in Poona, but I was not happy to be away from my family. I was being moved from one place to another like bhed-bakri, cattle. I was disoriented and did not understand what was happening.

My mother-in-law, Neeno, was not a nice woman. Bahut kharab thi. She used to make me do the housework like sweeping and mopping the house, washing the clothes and utensils, filling water pots, grinding the spices and cooking the food, and even taking care of the younger brothers and sisters of Ramlal. It was a lot of work for me at a time when I did not know how to do half the things I was being put through. I tried to recollect how my mother did it.

I did not know how to make a curry, so my mother-in-law would instruct me from her reclined position on a khaat, charpoy. She would not move an inch. She had a habit of shouting instead of talking. It always made me nervous. I would spoil things by forgetting to salt the curry or add too much spice.

We did not even speak the same language. I used to speak in our pede ki boli – the language of our Kanjarbhat community. The language is a mix of Rajasthani, Marathi and Hindi. Neeno used to speak in the rustic tongue of the bedias. At that time I did not know who the bedias were. There was already a communication gap between us, which made dealing with her worse. Sometimes I wished she would just die in her sleep.

At night, when I had to serve her a glass of hot milk to induce sleep, I would find her already asleep. For a minute, I would stare at her face, hoping that a stone on the ground would make me stumble and spill the milk on her doughy face. I could leave her peacefully to sleep, but I got my revenge by waking her up to remind her that she had ordered for the milk to help her sleep better.

She used to watch over me at all times. I could see it in her eyes that she was waiting for me to grow up. As if she would get rid of me when I did. Right now, all she was doing was taking pity at my diminutive size and intellect, saying, Bacchi hai abhi. She is just a child.

Before I could react to her taunts, my father-in-law, Chhedi Lal, would step in and calm her. He was a nice man. He used to bring fruits for us. He would speak to me politely. He treated me with a kindness that was rare to be seen in a man. Everyone I had known so far was bad.

I may have been a child, but my childhood was replaced with womanhood. Every time my mother-in-law taunted me for being a child, I felt a current rushing in my spine. My posture would become firm and erect. I grew tall, both in my limbs and in my thoughts: Bacchi nahi hoon main. I am not a child. I could think it, but had still not gathered the courage to utter it.

This was partly because I had not seen anything else to know any better. I was shipped from my parents' house to this new environment, where I was not allowed to step out of the house. I was growing up in a cage that was slowly shrinking.

One day, we stepped out for a picnic in a garden. There was a white marble structure in the backdrop. It was quite beautiful to look at. No one told me what it was. I also did not ask anyone. We did not go inside the building. We just sat on the ground and ate, while Ramlal's siblings played. I did not play because I was no longer considered a child. I had to sit and watch. Back then, I did not know what the Taj Mahal was, and that we lived near it. Love had not grazed my cheek. If it was in the air of Agra, it certainly never came knocking on my door.

I was in Ramlal's house till I was twelve or thirteen, I think. I cannot be sure – you see, I am not educated. I did not keep track of time, and memory eludes me. Ramlal is also dead now. His sister Cheenu lives here in Bow Bazaar. I meet her sometimes. Several years ago, when she told me Ramlal had died due to a liver failure, I thought to myself, Accha hua, ek paapi toh mara! Good, at least one sinner died.

Khair, anyway, one day, and it must have been some day, I was taken to Calcutta by train. My so-called good-for-nothing husband was left at home. I did not feel anything for him when I was being escorted away. Why were we travelling to Calcutta? I did not even know where we were going. Nothing was ever told to me in advance. For most of my life, it has been like that. Touch and go.

Ramlal's mother and father accompanied me. When we were in the train, I was so nervous about where they were taking me that I felt a hot fluid flowing from my legs. I thought I was urinating in fear. I ran to the bathroom and checked. It was blood. I knew what this meant. In our house in Poona, when my sister Babbo menstruated, she had to stay out of the house. Her menstrual dress – a lehenga, blouse and a long piece of cloth – was washed and kept in an earthen pot. She would have to wear the same dress for five or seven days. Food was served to her outside the house. She had to sleep away from everyone, on a gunnysack. She was not to touch any kaccha bartan, clean utensils or people. Her bleeding was a sign of her impurity. My sister had told me that it would happen to me as well and I was not to panic.

Ek maili aurat ek bhatki ladki se behtar hai. An impure woman is better than a clueless girl, Babbo laughed.

I was an impure woman now. I could not do anything to conceal it. I walked back into the compartment and sat in a corner, sucking on a pickled lemon.

Calcutta

WE ARRIVED IN THE BOW BAZAAR TRAM RASTA. MY MOTHER-IN-LAW had a daughter, Pushpa, who lived in a building with no name. Its number was the address – do sau unahtar. 269. It was afternoon; everyone was asleep in the building.

We walked into the narrow, dark alley leading to the decrepit building. We climbed the unlit stairs into a corridor. We entered a room. I rested in a corner. In the evening, after I woke up from a short nap, I found myself alone in the room, walking out to the sounds of musical instruments and ghungroos. I stepped out of the room and saw there were several rooms across with doors open. Young girls were singing and dancing and giggling. Yeh kya jagah hai? What is this place? I had never seen anything like this before.

Children were bawling in a corner, men were milling in front of the doors, the air reeked of the strong scent of flowers and incense. There was something harmonious even in the chaos in this new place, as if I knew I had come to a house I would prefer to all the other houses I had lived in so far. It was alien, but it also felt safe within the hubbub of melodies, stringing the air with a light touch of effervescence. All the girls were dazzling, with their slender bodies and mellifluous voices. I was shocked by how strangely seductive and unreal this world was. No one looked undesirable, even though all of them were not particularly beautiful in one way, but in so many other ways through their striking costumes, white-powdered make-up and shiny red lipstick. They all looked ready for a wedding, or a mela. Who would not find them attractive?

And me, I was such an alhad. Bumpkin. What was I doing here? How would I fit in?

Arre re re re, what is this? Pushpa said when she saw me.

She spotted the bloodstains on my saree. She gave me fresh clothes, but did not ask me to keep a social distance like in my house in Poona.

This was the first time I was meeting Pushpa. At first, Neeno and Pushpa gossiped about taking me to another place. I heard them say Sonagachi. I did not know who lived there. It was only then that I found out who my mother-in-law and her family were. My mother-in-law trafficked girls. It was her dhanda, profession, what the bednis did. Bedias travelled from less-developed villages to towns and cities, serving the rich as labourers. It was mostly the women who were hired for household work. Men were employed in the fields. Later, as the bednis began to offer pleasure and entertainment, they also began to earn more and control their families. Men came second in the pecking order. Soon, it was a prosperous sign for them to have more daughters than sons. The bednis who did not want their own daughters to do the dirty work began trafficking girls by procuring them from as far as possible, travelling through the west of the country and even up north to Kashmir – where they preferred fair skin over other shades, although a lot of the bednis who willingly got into the profession were deeply tanned in the hot central climate of UP and Bihar. Neeno's family picked up young girls from poor families and trained them to serve as naachne-gaanewali, courtesans, and as kamaanewalis, sex workers. So my marriage was a sham! I only found that out then in the building, where the mahaul – ambience – had already made me feel freer.

I had still not realized when Neeno must have seen me in Gullo's house. Why was I chosen? I was the least smart of all my sisters. But I could not betray my luck. So I did not ask too much about what they intended to do with me. I think they wanted to get rid of me by selling me in a brothel in Sonagachi. I did not know what a brothel was. They could not sell me, as it turned out. Meri kismat acchi thi. Luck was on my side.

Neeno and Pushpa consulted some men, who said there was no great price for a girl who was not a virgin. Nabaalik ladki ki demand zyada thi. Virgins were preferred. She wanted to sell me as a young woman by lying that I was still a virgin. Some women advised Neeno and Pushpa to be truthful about me. It could backfire.

I am handing you to Pushpa for an amount of money in exchange. You have to work for her till she recovers it, Neeno said to me.

I used to do as they said. Utho toh utho, baitho toh baitho. Get up and sit down on their instructions. I did ask them out of courtesy – where have you brought me?

Neeno told me to keep quiet and do as Pushpa said from there on. I nodded.

The next morning, I was sitting in front of an ustad, Ashfaq. He had a harmonium and a stern command to open my mouth and sing as loud as him. *Sa-re-ga*, it went. I sang like Neelkamal, my goat. I hardly ever spoke – how was I going to sing?

No one was impressed. The ustad picked a paan from a brass tashtari, chewed it till it became a liquid that filled his cheeks and then sang with a guttural twang, juggling the red juice in his mouth as if it was lubricating his throat as the words bubbled up.

Sa-re-ga.

Sa-re-ga, my faint voice trembled.

What a waste! Pushpa said, spitting chewed betel nut in a peekdaan, spittoon.

I wished the ustad would use the spittoon too and not open his fountain mouth that sprinkled red spittle all over. It looked like blood was oozing out of his mouth. He was dying as he sang. I was too frightened to imitate him.

I feared they would take me to Sonagachi. I had to be good at this. Pushpa used to spend half her time in Bow Bazaar and half her time in Sonagachi. She never took me there. I was not ready for there or here.

A more foul-mouthed but good teacher was ustad Bashir Khan.

Haraamzaadi, suar ki bacchi, taal samajh mein nahi aata kya? Bastard, piglet, can't you follow the rhythm? he used to shout at me, beating the tabla and handing me the tanpura to sync in teen taal. Initially, I did not understand anything at all. What is going on? Yeh sab kya hai?

Oh, and suar reminds me, I had to cook suar ka gosht in Ramlal's house. I did not eat it. I hated even cooking it. I found it repulsive. Pigs used to be so filthy to look at – keechad mein ghoomte, tatti khaate, roaming in sludge, eating shit. We, my mother and sisters, did not eat suar. Later I heard that even uttering the word suar was a sin in Islam. I can only imagine Bashir Khan's irritation with me. He was a sociable man otherwise.

Another ustad began to train me in kathak. I think his name was Krishna guruji. He would utter the bol – *Dha Ge Na Ti Na Ke Dhi Na Dha* – saying it was Keherwa taal. He would clap and ask me to stomp my feet in sync with his utterances. Here, I did fine. Herding goats, I used to be jumpy in the fields. I had a natural rhythm in my body, you can say. I knew in my heart that I could do this. I felt dancing was easier than singing raags. Singing could

take years to learn. Dance was not so strict, so formal. It worked
on the rhythm of the moving body, not the voice that had to be
produced from within. I was never the talkative one. It took me
a longer time to sing. My body, however, responded instantly to
music. Soon, I was able to follow several other taals on my feet.
The guruji taught us the styles of Hindi-film dancers. He spoke of
Bela Bose, Padmini, Ragini, Rani, Laxmi Chhaya, Minoo Mumtaz,
Helen and Kumkum. I thought he was telling me about his former
students. I would only find out later who they were: Hindi-film
heroines.

Pushpa noticed that I was a quick learner. I was not such a waste
of her money after all. Neeno had left me with her and returned to
Agra. I did not see Neeno again for a long time. The singing and
dancing training lasted for a few months.

I used to apply a red tika and kiss the ghungroos before wearing
them every morning for the riyaaz, music practice, as I saw the other
girls do the same. I think initially everything I was doing was by
imitating those around me. I thought that was the best way to blend
in and become invisible. So that no one would single me out for
some other kitchen work. I detested that work now because of my
experience with Neeno.

The Basant raag was commonly taught. The ustads would say it
was easier to teach. I could not tell one raag from another. I tried
singing with dedication. One of the first melodies that I had learnt
by heart was 'Hasta hua noorani chehra'. Two girls used to sing it
as a duet. Seeing another girl accompany me gave me the courage
I needed.

I used to hear the name of Ghalib a lot. The ustads would
mention Mirza Ghalib while talking about some ghazal.

Yeh ghazal Ghalib ki likhi hui hai, Ghalib has written this ghazal,
an ustad would say, trying to teach me the lyrics of a song.

One time I told the ustad Ashfaq, Bahut acchi hai, par samajh mein nahi aayi. It's lovely, but I couldn't follow it. Why do you not call him also, so that he can tell us what his ghazal means, I said.

The ustad laughed and said Ghalib had died a long time ago.

Oh, ho, I said, all these bhaari-bhaari, high-brow, ghazals must have taken a toll on his health. Let us not practise his ghazal then, I said. Most of Ghalib's ghazals had complex Urdu words. I found another ghazal simpler to rote.

A ghazal I was taught was: '*Humare baad andhera rahega mehfil mein, bahut charagh jalaoge roshni ke liye.*' Darkness will consume the gathering when I am gone, you will unsuccessfully light several lamps to illuminate it.

I loved the words of this ghazal. The sadness of its poetry struck a chord. It reflected my own misery in some way that I was too young to explain but felt deeply. I had mastered '*Hasta hua noorani chehra*' and this ghazal. I was confident of these two particular songs because together they mirrored the happy and sad versions of me. The chirpy melody was for the raees, patrons, who came for entertainment. The ghazal expressed my personal feelings. Ustad Ashfaq told me that an anonymous poet had written this ghazal. That resonated even more with me. I was also a nobody – I felt anonymous here.

I learnt the meaning of Urdu words through these songs that I was taught. I would ask the ustad for the meaning to interpret it with feeling. Some girls would do alaaps and taans, vocal flourishes, and all other kinds of classical singing harkats, movement of notes, which I could not master. Soon, I was told that I was prepared to perform in front of an audience. By this time I had watched the other girls in the kotha perform in front of men. I followed their haav-bhaav, mannerisms and studied different styles of make-up and hair.

The patrons would sit on a gaddi on one side of the room. On the other side, the harmonium ustad, the tabla player and the sarangiwala would be seated. The mujrewali would sit in the centre of the room, her back to the musicians and facing the patrons. The men came loaded with cash, to drink, watch and shower on the girls. The girl could sing anything she liked in the beginning, any popular Hindi-film melody to excite the crowd. The men would follow it up with a request for a ghazal as soon as the alcohol began to intoxicate them. From then, it would become a quieter, more intimate gathering that could go on for hours into the night.

In those days, there was a fixed rate for a performance. The party, or a group of men, never more than five or so, since the rooms were also very small, would together have to pay a sum of fifty rupees for a sitting. If they liked the girl, they could shower her with more money. If they asked her to dance, they would pay more. The musicians would split twenty rupees as their cut and the performer got the rest. The extra money was always a bonus that she could split with the musicians if she favoured them. This way, a girl had a set of her own loyal saazinde, musicians.

I saw all this happen. When I performed, the money did not come into my hands. Pushpa sat in the room to watch me. Pushpa said that money would be used to clear my debts for the amount that Neeno was paid.

This went on for two or three years, I am not sure. It took forever for the debt to clear.

Pushpa took me to the dargah of Sabir piya in Kaliyar, Haridwar. An annual mela used to be held there, where classical singers used to sing and mujrewalis used to dance in tents.

When we got there, we were allotted a tent at the far end of the premise, where the snake charmers and the street performers were given space. I realized immediately that it was going to be a flop show. A bedni from Agra and three musicians were with us. The good tents were booked and given to the illustrious bais from Calcutta, Bombay and Delhi.

The first day was dull. Few people turned up. We danced to *'Chadhti jawani meri chaal mastani'*, *'Bindiya chamkegi'*, *'Honthon pe aisi baat'*, *'Koi shehri babu'*, *'Kaanta laga'*, all such chaalu, flashy songs.

Most men were interested in the eunuchs who performed in this shady area. I did not know they were eunuchs. Their dance was more titillating than ours. Their clothes were flashier. Their confident smiles, you could say, more welcoming. We were young girls, trained and following certain decorum. They were not like us. I would say they danced more freely than us.

Yeh kaun hai? I asked an ustad.

Yeh toh hijde hain, he said and laughed.

Till then, I had no concept of who hijdas were.

Woh kya hota hai? Who are they?

Woh aadmi hain, he said. They are men.

Hain? I said. Itne khoobsurat. So beautiful.

A hijda befriended us. I was able to bond with him. We ate breakfast together and discussed our lives. He would entertain us by showing us some great, acrobatic steps like the people who perform in a circus. I tried to imitate him, but I was not too good at it. His moves were intricate, if a little too daring for us.

The hijda used to talk brazenly, khul ke.

Laaj, sharam kis kaam ka? he said. What use is modesty? Paise kiske milte hain? What do we get money for, he mocked us, shimmying his flat cleavage and making us laugh, because we had the real thing and we were covering it.

We could see why the crowd preferred the hijdas. They shamelessly flirted with the men, grabbed money from their hands, teased them, touched them – all with the certainty that we women could not. We had to maintain a distance because we did not want the men to jump on us. Kood padhte hain.

And if the men jumped on the hijdas, they knew how to take them on. We would never be able to do that.

The crowd used to give us one rupee, two rupees. This was not a ten-rupee crowd. It was a tough, mostly poor crowd. On the second day, after my bath, I went to the dargah to pay my respects.

Salaam, I said, to the baba's tomb. I prayed, saying, Aap meri laaj rakh lo. Guard my honour.

Inspired by the hijda, I began to dance more freely. I knew the kathak steps that we used to mix with filmy steps, but now was the chance to break from the rules and add some extra zing. The crowd a began to gather. The music did not stop. I danced like a woman in a trance, but I also knew my limits. I did not interact with the crowd like the hijdas, however I made my performance more skilful. The money flowed. It formed an anthill before my eyes. The sarangi ustad filled the sarangi khol with money.

I was too young to know how well I did. There were no rewards. I was a slave, so I did not see the colour of money come into my hands. Pushpa looked after the sarangi khol with notes and coins. I got nothing.

But I learnt something important from this mela. I saw how so many people came to see us. They were mostly common, ordinary folk. I saw how they tossed currency notes at us. I would notice the notes falling near our feet. I could not pick them up and run. I felt so rich and yet so helpless!

A young man fell in love with me after seeing my dance performance. I was dancing all night. When the azaan broke and the crows cawed, we stopped. In the morning, the young man brought breakfast for me: halwa, puri and chai. I was tired, but also hungry. I ate and slept till afternoon.

When I woke up, he was sitting outside the tent.

What is your name? he asked.

Rekha, I said self-consciously. No one had ever asked my name itne pyaar se, with such tenderness. Gullo had always called me Dulari – my favourite. I was used to being called iterations of it by

my sisters: Dullo, Dulli. Telling a stranger my name made me feel
shy, as if I was giving a part of myself to him.

He told me his name, but I have forgotten it now. I remember he
told me he was a choodiwala, a bangle maker. We became friends.
He came to see my performance every night, for ten nights. He
would feed me breakfast, talk and leave. I liked him a lot, but I
did not have any romantic feelings for him. I could see that he
was glassy-eyed. I just did not have the time for love. Or I was just
beginning to feel the first flush of true love. The concept of love was
still new to me.

One day he asked, When are you leaving, and which train will
you be taking?

I told him the date, time and name of the train. I did not suspect
anything fishy about him. When we performed in the tent, we had
fans and stalkers. By now, I could judge men with my instinct. Some
goons had also started following us. They would insist to go with
me to bathe in a holy nehar, canal. I had told the ustads about it.
You just say yes, said one aged ustad. We know how to give them
chakma, the slip, beta.

I had told the goons that I would go with them. I gave them a
date. They did not trust me, so some of their men kept an eye on us.
What I had done was I had told them to pick me up one day after
the ten-day mela was over. The ustads and I had planned to escape
on the tenth night.

As we left, a goon followed us. The ustad told me not to worry.
By the time the goon would inform his boss, we would have left.

The choodiwala did not intimidate me, so I was frank with him.

On the tenth night, when I had boarded the train, he came to see
me with a box filled with colourful glass bangles.

Itne saare, so many, I said with happiness. My eyes brimmed
with tears.

I would have made more if I had the time, he said.

He then gave me a small box. It looked like it contained something special. When I opened it, I saw that he had made red glass bangles with my name engraved on them. These were truly special and required great artistry.

He did not want anything from me. He did not even make promises to meet again. He was just happy to see that his gift had made me smile.

In that moment, when the train pulled away from the platform, I watched him waving goodbye. I felt a strange, heavy weight sit on my heart. But I didn't understand what it meant. Uss time dil-vil kya hota hai, kya pata tha! I didn't know what love was then! Had I disembarked, would I have found true love? Kya jaane kya naam tha uska, yaad nahi aa raha. What was his name? I can't seem to recollect.

The ten days in Kaliyar were a hit. I do not know how well I did in comparison to the other bais, but since I do not know how to count money and have never seen so much of it, I can safely say we did well. I was wearing new bangles, and they felt more precious than money.

In those years, when Pushpa took me to melas, I learnt a lot by observing how important money was to these traffickers and how I was just a means to it. In fact, I was going to be disposable the minute I rebelled. The profession was giving me the ammunition I needed to grow. I was thinking of ways to break away, but I did not have any concrete plans. How was I going to get away from there? I was never allowed to step out of the building. Someone was always watching me.

My freedom came in the dark.

Once, there was a blackout in Calcutta. Everyone was fleeing. People were saying there was a war somewhere on the border. I heard there was an Emergency. I heard of the India–China border.

I heard of the India–Bangladesh border. What did I know of these places? There was already a war going on in my own head.

Let us leave, Pushpa said.

No, I am not going back with you, I said.

What, are you mad? You will die.

I want to die. It is better than living with you.

What an ungrateful haraamzaadi, she said.

She asked me why I was being stubborn. I said I did not want to go back to that house again. It was just my zid. I did not want to go back to my past. I liked it here.

You will rot here; you will die.

Apne naseeb se, I said. I was using my mother's words to fortify my fate.

Pushpa feared for her life. She fled to Agra. I did not care about dying, just as I had not fully lived yet.

I danced in the dark. I used to light up the kotha with candles and perform. That ghazal I loved, '*Humare baad andhera rahega mehfil mein, bahut charagh jalaoge roshni ke liye.*' It became my signature closing song. Those who wanted to be entertained came even when the war was overhead. We did not hear any bullets. We did not see bombs explode. We heard sirens. It sent people scampering in all directions. Those who wanted to dance with death came to the kotha. If they were going to die, they wanted to be surrounded by the best things in life – whisky, women and music. Marta kya nahi karta? What doesn't a dying man do?

Khoob mujra kiya, khoob nachi. I danced a lot on those dark nights. Like Waheeda Rehman in *Guide*. The words of '*Aaj phir jeene ki tamanna hai*' resonated:

Kaanton se kheench ke yeh aanchal
Tod ke bandhan baandhe payal

Koyi na roko dil ki udaan ko
Dil woh chala … aa aa aa
Aaj phir jeene ki tamanna hai
Aaj phir marne ka irada hai …

In the blackout, my naseeb was going to shine. I knew that now I could keep the money. It was all mine. It was a risk I took, but my whole life had been without a plan – so I had not a thing to worry. By this time, I had become confident that I could survive on my skills as a performer. This was the first time in my life I was touching money, licking my fingers to count it. It was a giddy rush. I also realized how much power I could wield over my own life with this money. The blackout lasted about ten days, I think. I had made money the size of a quilt to snuggle into.

What is it about qayamat ke din, the end of the world, that makes men rush towards it like bees trying to embrace a flower? All sorts of men came to watch me – policemen, party workers, politicians, businessmen, goons. Oh, once, some Bangladeshi freedom fighters also came. One of them was called Mujibur, I think. I did not care who came – everyone was welcome. I was doing nothing other than performing. More than the money, I was in control. I had seen money before. Now, I owned it. How should I describe that feeling? When the poor are no longer weak. Money boosts confidence like nasha, intoxication. That is how I felt. The nasha of money had just begun. It was yet to consume me. I thought to myself: Kya main itna saara paisa kamati hoon? Is this how much money I make? I cried in joy. My heart felt happiness – it was a totally new feeling. I decided that if Pushpa returned, I would rent a separate room and perform solo.

It was during this time that I had my first brush with a goonda. A short, dark man with a decent face by the name of Munna would come to the kotha. He grew fond of me and spent a lot of money on my mujras. One day he asked me to marry him.

I flat out refused, saying I was married. He said he would give me a better life.

Where, I asked?

My place, he said.

Where is that?

Anywhere you want it to be, he said.

But where will you take me now? Do you have a home here?

No, he said.

Then how will you give me a grihasti, a parivar – a household, a family? You are a small-time crook, what good will my life be with you?

Aye, Rekha, he said, pulling out a pistol. Do not upset me, I will take you by force.

Theek hai, I said, take me, but where? Even my husband left me here!

I called a few girls in the kotha and told them I am going with Munna. They stared quietly at him. One of the girls, Seema, said, Take me also. Another girl said the same. Yet another girl said, Yeh kya leke jayega, main kab se wait kar rahi hoon. Where will he take us, I have been waiting forever. Everyone laughed. Munna did not know what to say next. He was outwitted.

He came back after a few days, but his attitude had changed. He was softer. He spoke politely and tried to be a friend. He must have understood to not curb my freedom in the kotha. One time, I fell ill. He took me to a doctor. I trusted him. That made him feel better about himself. He used to loot goods trains in Dhanbad. He would disappear for months on end. Many years later, I heard he was killed in an encounter with the police.

The blackout period was brief. Pushpa came back after a few months. She immediately asked me for my earnings.

Kitne kamaye? How much did you earn? she asked.

Kyon? Why? I said.

La, give, she said.

Kyon, kis liye? Why, what for? I said. I hid the money in a few spots, but I also stored a roll in my blouse. We women know that our bodies are the safest place to hide money. I had learnt that by watching my mother.

Pushpa did not try to touch me. She could see the resentment on my face. She was going to have to find another way to tackle me. I did not budge. I was a different person now. A few months were all it took to hold the reins of my life in my own hands. I was not going to give in.

Tunay toh yahan gaane gaaye, mujra kiya; paise toh humare hote hain, said Pushpa. You have sung songs and danced on our time; the money belongs to us.

Nahi, paise toh mere hote hain, I said. I earned the money.

She did not know how to react. She had to start anew, without me. I had grown up in these years in the kotha. From a slave, I had turned into a rebel. I rented an empty room on the same floor to compete and defy her. She got a new girl, a short but pretty one called Chitra. I was no match for her in terms of looks, but the girl had to be trained first, so I had an advantage over her. The other girls in the kotha – Meera, Meena, Nirmala, Kapuri, Seema – had become my friends. I went out shopping with them to Bada Bazaar. Buying Prem Nagar and Manchali sarees and jewellery, all of my own choice, was thrilling. There were new silk sarees to be draped, new shades of lipstick to apply, new anklets to wear. We even wore Western clothes. I tried on a pair of jeans and dark sunglasses, and posed for a photographer in a studio. It was so thrilling. We went to the movies, ate in restaurants. Seema and I smoked a cigarette in a bathroom. She used to smoke cigarettes that had a chocolatey flavour. She asked me to take a puff. I was wide-eyed about vices.

No, I do not do such things, I said.

I am telling you, she said, try it first.

I took a few puffs and immediately started coughing.

She snatched the cigarette from me and said, You are right, this is not for you.

She opened the door and pushed me out of the bathroom.

I laughed and felt free, but my mind was also now always preoccupied with the thought of where I belonged. Should I be enjoying any of this? This short burst of freedom always meant something bad was just around the corner. I had begun to question if feeling free or happy were emotions that were real at all.

Where was I from? Where did my parents live? I had no address, no recollection of where exactly our hut stood. I knew it was somewhere in Pimpri, Poona, but where precisely, I did not know. How could I trace them? In all these years, there had been no mention of my family's name; no one ever came to see me in Agra. Did they even know that I was in Calcutta now? In a kotha!

As for me, I never got the time to grieve my separation from them. I did not get a moment's respite to think about them, to cry, to miss, to yearn for my mother, my family that had forsaken me. My sisters – how were they doing? My little brother, who was growing up to protect us – how was he?

Now, when I had money, it gave me the strength to think about them. It gave me the freedom to look for them. It gave me the voice to speak up and enquire. I could now face Pushpa and ask her to trace them. I could even pay her to do so.

Pushpa stopped speaking to me. She would not tell me anything. She then began to harass me. She would not let me use the common bathroom. She would yell and quarrel and pick fights with me for no reason. She tried to beat me. I fought back. I had seen fights between girls before. I was prepared for it. If she raised a hand, so did I. We pulled each other's hair.

In the evenings, she would not allow young men through the passage in the corridor towards my room. No one turned up at my door.

She began to employ goons from the streets to stalk me if I went out. They would hang around the stairs and the corridor to intimidate me. I could not step out of my room fearing them. I would keep myself locked in. I often took shelter in the company of my friends in the evening. Pushpa began alienating them from me, one by one, by gossiping. This went on for several months.

It broke me. I realized I did not have anyone standing up for me. I decided I would give up and leave. Was this not what she wanted? She wanted me to leave. If she could not control me, she was using all her might to throw me out.

One morning, I stepped out, went down the building and was looking for a rickshaw when Pushpa understood I was going to the Howrah railway station. She came down and dragged me back inside, saying I could not leave.

Why will you not even let me leave? I shouted.

Where will you go, what will you do? she said. You will be torn to pieces by this world in seconds. Do you know who you are?

I was aware of my reputation. I had earned it. I was a baiji.

Khaangi ho, randi ho, she shouted. Randi, she screamed and hurled abuses at me.

A crowd gathered, attracted by the booming, harsh and loud sound of that one word. I knew what it meant. But in her screaming voice it came out like a radio announcement. R A N D I.

It sounded horrible. I knew it had the power to stop any man in his tracks and make him stare. It also made everyone stare accusingly at the person who was being shouted at.

I was being called a randi. I was being disgraced. I was being humiliated in broad daylight in front of a crowd.

She pulled at my saree. I felt naked, being harassed in public. The word was shrill, and loud and deafening. Randi. That is how people saw us. I was not a prostitute, but how does any man know better than to judge us as one when one of our own is calling us a whore? A randi.

That was the first time someone had called me a name that I was not. In a public place, in an open street, where strangers were walking by, most of whom stopped to stare at me. Their eyes burnt into me. My skin crawled. The light in the sky was too bright, too harsh. Being dragged back from under the clear blue sky was like being pulled into a pool of darkness, into a pitch-dark cave, where I belonged, where women like me belonged.

It was a worse feeling than leaving. To be forcefully pulled back from escaping, with the humiliation that I was no ordinary woman. I was branded a whore. I was stripped of any dignity I might have had as a nobody. This was a sickening realization, that I had no place in the world when I had just about mustered up enough courage to step out into it.

I tumbled into grief and longing. I missed my parents, my sisters and my home. I did not feel good about being independent any more. It was a burden to be free with no mooring.

Pushpa called a police officer from Lal Bazaar thana to scare and threaten me. He said I could not leave. If I ran, I would be caught and jailed for stealing.

I could not move out of the kotha. I was being forced to perform. I was depressed. I was in no mood to smile. They had systematically robbed me of my identity and left me soulless. I was being enslaved again. Some months went by in complete numbness. Then, just like that, I snapped out of it. I woke up.

I decided to do the mujras and steal money right in front of Pushpa. I faked a smile and sang. When the raees showered notes,

I collected them and passed it on to the ustads, but managed to slip a few notes under my seat. I usually got more money showers when I danced. I would quickly grab flying notes while pirouetting with my hands up in the air, crush them and slip them inside my bra. Later, I would straighten those notes out in the bathroom and stash them in a secret place.

A lanky young man from Howrah used to visit us for the mujras. He said he worked at the railway station. I do not know why I felt like I could trust him, but I could rely on my instincts. For me, the name Howrah was a railway station. The bridge over the Hooghly river was a passage to escape from the city.

Listen, can you please get me a train ticket to Poona? I said to him.

He was a kind fellow. He did not say a word then. He understood. He could feel my desperation. He did not want something in return. He never demanded anything from me.

After a few days, he said that he had arranged for a ticket. I was ecstatic. But how would I get to the station? I did not know the way.

He instructed me. He said everyone knew where Howrah station was. Just hop on to a rickshaw. He said the train was at eight in the evening. He said he would stand at the main gate with the ticket.

What else could I do? I had to trust him. I do not even remember his name now.

On the day of my escape, I folded two sarees into a small peti and told Pushpa that I was leaving.

I stormed into her room. I challenged her.

I am leaving, I said. Stop me if you can. You have tortured me a lot. I can withstand a few more blows if you try. Come and get me if you can. I dare you to lay a hand on me.

I do not know what happened to Pushpa then. She did not pounce on me. She laughed.

Chal jaa, she said.

She knew me better than I did, I guess. She knew this was not the end of my story.

I was stunned.

Fine, I said. You wait and watch. I will be back. I will take a room across yours and make you sorry for yourself.

Jaa, jaa, she said. I know.

She was giving me up without a fight. How could this be so easy? My legs began to wobble with uncertainty. I had to make a quick dash before she could say another word.

I ran out, went downstairs, hollered at a rickshaw-wala: Howrah station.

Those two words took an eternity to reach him. Those magic words were like a spell that broke the illusion. I was free to leave.

It was seven in the evening. I had an hour. The rickshaw-wala must have sped. I kept telling him jaldi, jaldi, fast fast, fearful that I was being followed. I did not trust Pushpa. I think she laughed because she knew I would not get too far in the evening. I had never been out alone after dark. I wanted to laugh as well. My eyes were brimming with tears. Happiness was mixed with sorrow, with fear.

What if the guy had told Pushpa about my plans? What if he was standing at the gate with a policeman to arrest me? All kinds of strange thoughts began to cloud my mind, despite the excitement I felt at the thought that I was getting away from the stranglehold of these horrible, exploitative people.

When I reached Howrah station, sure enough, the guy was standing with the ticket. I spotted him from the rickshaw, like it was a high throne from where I could survey the busy thoroughfare.

I would have hugged him had I any sense of gratitude. Human kindness was so rare to come by, I did not know how to react to it.

You will really go? he asked.

Yes, I said.

Will you come back? he asked.

No, I said.

I asked him to escort me to the compartment where my seat was. He did that. What he did for me gave me strength, courage, confidence that I was not alone if I asked for help.

We seldom ask someone for help, fearing that the person may have an ulterior motive. This man had a sense of urgency on his face that he was in it for the good and nothing else. I must have read it on his face. It was a sincere, honest face.

In the kotha, we observe how men look at us. We can tell in a group which one is there for the entertainment and which one is there for more. Those looking for more usually get less. The ones not looking for more are likely to get lucky. He was one of those. I was in too much of a hurry to leave, or I would have likely fallen in love with him for the simple reason that he had been kind to me. Men also like us when we are at our most vulnerable. But that did not seem to cross his mind. He did not profess any undying affection for me. When he asked me if I would return, it did not seem like he wanted me to come back for him. He did not smile out of courtesy. That gave him the character of nobility I now admired. A man not here to please anybody. I was somewhat like that in the beginning. Trying to hold on to my dignity in a profession that did not give it.

I wish I had remembered his name. I must have forgotten it in his kindness. Strangers leave us with so much to thank for that they forget to remind us of their names. He did not take any money for the ticket. He was an angel for me.

Here I was again. In another train. On another journey. Unclear where it would take me. Only this time, I was alone. I was on my own. That gave me both fear and courage. If I could do this, I could achieve anything. If I could find my parents, I was, like my mother said, shaping my own destiny, retracing my way back home, to be reunited with my family.

Poona

THE TRAIN WAS TILL KALYAN STATION. WHEN I REACHED THERE, I went to the waiting room to freshen up. I asked a woman to keep an eye on my peti, luggage. She said yes. When I returned from the bathroom, my peti with the two sarees was gone. I had fortunately tucked some money into my blouse earlier. I asked people about the train to Poona. I did not buy a ticket. I boarded the train and asked a passenger to inform me when the train halted at the Pimpri station. I knew from my childhood that we lived in Pimpri. I had heard the name several times. It stayed with me like a wound, never to heal, always to remind on touch that beneath the surface was a deep blue wound of my innocent days, when memory had not formed yet, and can only be reached by intuition.

There used to be a Roxy hotel on the highway. I used to go there as a kid to buy sweets. It is still there. Next to the Bank of India branch where I now have an account. I can buy all the sweets I want now.

I walked around, asking people for directions to the hotel. When I found it, I asked the manager at the counter if he knew me. He said he could vaguely recollect. I told him about my sisters, my parents and my hut. He knew us. He showed me the way to my mother's hut that was on the side of a road.

I did not know if I would recognize my mother. But would she recognize me? I had grown up from a little girl into a woman. I saw her sitting outside her hut in the afternoon. She was filling some pots with water.

The shopkeeper said, That is your mother.

I immediately teared up. I called out, Maa!

She stood up to look at me. I walked across the road. I waited for a second for her to recognize me. She did not blink.

Dulari, she said. Dulari, my dear one. The dear one she had let go so easily.

She instantly hugged me and began to cry. I was inconsolable too. I was back home. In my mother's arms. It was a reunion that seemed to last forever. She would not stop crying. She would not let go of me as if we were saying goodbye.

My sisters gathered around me. They gave me water to drink and took me inside the hut. I could see that nothing had changed for them. They were still very poor and lived very frugally. I was a city girl now. I had seen the fast life, the big life. I could not bear to see their condition and not think about how I could make it better. My family was happy to see me, but here I was, one more mouth to feed. I was carrying five-hundred rupees on me. I gave it to my mother. She was shocked to see so much money.

Where did you get this from? she asked.

I told her I would explain it later. She could have it all.

I spent a month doing nothing. I stayed at home, trying to figure out what to do with my life. I had become restless, as I had seen how I could make money. The more time spent here in penury was more time wasted not overcoming it.

Where is your husband? my sisters asked.

I told everyone what had happened. This made my mother cry even more. She said she would get me remarried. I could live close to her. Did she want to sell me again? I doubted her intentions. I was worried for days. One day, when she pestered me too much, I climbed atop a water tower and said I would jump if she insisted on getting me married.

Will your in-laws not come looking for you here now? she asked.

Let them come – I will see, I said.

They were the least of my fears. My fears were more that we would perish in poverty. My younger sisters were growing up. They needed to be fed well and looked after. My younger sister Shanna was a thin, scrawny girl, like I used to be. She was fairer than me, prettier, with big, innocent brown eyes that had never seen anything outside the hut. She was wearing a dirty skirt torn at the hem. Her pigtails were tied in tattered ribbons. She reminded me of myself.

What do you want to do when you grow up? I asked her.

What do you mean? she replied.

As if no possibility existed outside the hut.

In that moment, I knew what I had to do. Just knowing that a world of happiness awaited her, that I could bring it to her, made my heart ache. This little girl can have it all, I thought. I will send her to school, I will arrange her marriage into a good family. I will give her everything I could not have. Her meaningless life gave me a mission. I have to go back, I thought.

Where is the money I gave you? I asked my mother.

I spent it on ration, clothes, she said.

I knew she was lying. I did not want to argue. My father was lying on a khaat, drunk and almost dead. We had never looked at him for answers.

Can you get me three-hundred rupees, at least? I asked.

She had given me a pair of silver earrings to wear when I had returned. I was wearing them and had not looked at them in a while.

I have a pair of earrings that you are wearing, she said.

I took them off and said she could sell them.

As I was doing so, I noticed I was wearing two thin gold bangles. In my distress, I had not paid any attention to myself. I took them off and handed them to her as well.

What do you need the money for? she asked.

I want to go back to the city and earn.

She tried to dissuade me by telling me that Pushpa would get me killed. I was undeterred.

Do not sell these, just pawn them in a shop, and get me the money. Do not worry, in one month I will make sure you have twice as much, I said.

Calcutta

Gullo did as I told her. I took the money, gave some to all my sisters and returned to Calcutta.

I think the train ticket cost me fifty rupees. I had one hundred rupees with me. And some small change for water and tea. My mother had packed me some rotis with my favourite lemon pickle for the journey. She cried a lot at the platform, saying I was being stupid. Not for a minute did I hesitate when I had this brainwave that I should return to Calcutta. What if Pushpa tried to get me arrested? Or sent goons to intimidate me?

Dekha jayega, I kept telling myself. I'll see when I get there.

I was not thinking it through. I was not trying to be brave. I was only resisting our poverty. I wanted my family to have the basic things in life. Food, clothes, shelter. I could get it for them. That was all I was aiming for. I did not for once think I was going to vanquish Pushpa or any other obstacle that came in my way. In fact, I wanted to step aside from any danger and make a new path for myself.

What was so brave or bold or fearless in a girl wanting to secure a little happiness and comfort for her poor family? I felt I could achieve it through hard work. Is this not what I had been doing so far? Had I not seen the fruits of my labour?

So I marched back to Calcutta like I was returning from a vacation. I had no idea what I would do. Should I go back to Pushpa? Should I stay in the same kotha? Should I look for another kotha? The long train journey was the perfect time to give it some thought. I looked out of the window, watching the world go by – and what went by was in the past and what was ahead was my future. It was that simple. The window looked like a blank, clean slate, where I could scrawl my destiny. I had set things in motion, now I had to plan for what I would do next.

When I reached Howrah station, the air was cool, the platform was chaotic as usual and my heart was pulsing at a normal rate. Everything around me began to feel familiar. Nothing looked out of place or alien any more. I could breathe an air of freedom, liberty. Azaadi!

I went to the cloakroom and locked my peti, suitcase. It had a saree I had borrowed from my mother. It was precious enough to be kept in a safe place before I could think about what to do next. I walked out of the station and saw that the crowd was scattered. It was not as busy as before. I hailed a taxi and went to the Kalighat temple to pray to Kali Ma.

Aye, Kali Ma, I said, tu mujhe apne sheher mein safal kar de, bas. O Mother Kali, give me a taste of success in your city.

I then went to building number ekyasi – 81. I was known in this kotha. The girls had heard of me before. I went and met the bariwala, the caretaker. His name was Inder bhaiya. He knew me from the kotha in building number 269.

Arre, he said, Rekha, tu?

As if his long-lost sister had returned.

I had run away, I said. I am back now. I need your help.

He understood everything without asking me details. Word travels fast in these places. Gossip would have had me killed and dumped in a drain by now. How I survived!

I explained to him what had happened. The girls began to gather. A few months must have passed since my disappearance from the scene. People would have forgotten about me, but not the girls when they saw competition returning. Some spoke to me in a friendly tone, some in horror and some in solidarity. I knew no one really cared.

Inder bhaiya, I said, I need to rent a room here, but I do not have the money to pay in advance right now. I will arrange for it in four days. I do not want a room at the end of the corridor. I want something in the middle. He nodded and arranged for a room to be opened. When I walked into the room, it felt as though it ended at the door itself. It was a small room. There was nothing inside. No bed, no lights, no earthen pot for water. The room was rented out to me at four hundred rupees a month. That was a steep amount. How could I give him the surety that I could pay the amount soon?

I remember that day very vividly. It was an election day. The streets were empty. I wondered how smoothly things were happening at this hour. I was able to move from one location to another with great speed, assembling basic essentials for the new room. It was as if Kali Ma had heard my prayers and had opened up the city for me.

With the hundred rupees I had, I went to the market and bought a bucket, a broom, a water pot, a few glasses, a chattai and a bedsheet to cover it. I spent all the money I had. In the evening, I took a bath in the common bathroom. I had not eaten anything all day. I had only a rupee and seventy-five paise left with me. I had tied the change to one end of my pallu. I got a cup of chai for twenty-five paise and a singara for twenty-five paise. I was going to relaunch myself in the market with barely a rupee's security to lean on. After filling my stomach with some fuel, I felt recharged.

The kotha is designed in such a way that the corridors look out on to the street. I came out of my room and began pacing the corridor, worrying about what was next. What would I do now? I untied my hair and began combing it, as if a solution would fall out of its dense folds. Just then Lal saab was crossing the street. Lal saab was the manager at Allahabad Bank.

He looked up and said to his friend Pandeyji, I think that is Rekha standing there. Lal saab was a slightly portly old man in his late sixties. He used glasses to look. Pandeyji reminded him that he was not wearing his glasses.

I do not need them to recognize her, he said.

How can you be so sure? said Pandeyji.

You should go and check. I will wait here, said Lal saab.

Pandeyji was surprised to find me. Lal saab and he used to be regular patrons at 269.

When Pandeyji asked me how come I was in this kotha, I tried to sound defensive.

Yes, why not? I said.

He smiled and said Lal saab was standing outside. That made me nervous.

That is fine, but where will I ask him to sit? I said. I do not have a gaddi or pillows. There is no fan or light in this room. I cannot welcome him here.

Do not worry about all that, he said. I will fetch him.

Lal saab came in. He sat on the chattai. He was a wise old man. He knew what had happened when I had left 269. He did not bring it up. I am so happy to see you again, he said. Let us get some sweets to celebrate.

He sent Pandeyji to fetch rasgulla and singara. When he tried to feed me a rasgulla, I began to weep. I could not control my tears any more. I was hungry. So I took a bite with relish. That bite might have

satiated a great many hungers within me. The hunger of any artiste is
to feed the imagination of the always-hungry audience. The opposite
was happening here. Lal saab's kindness was filling me up.

Eat, eat, he said. Arre, pagli, do not cry.

There was a softness in Lal saab's voice, almost berating me like a
father figure. To distract me, he asked me for a glass of water.

He drank it and said, Chal ek gaana suna de. Sing me a song.

No, I said. I do not want to sing.

Oh ho, just call the ustads, he said. We are already sitting on
the floor.

On his insistence, I went to Inder bhaiya and asked him to send his
servant, Ramu, across the tramline. The ustads used to sit on the side
of the road in the evenings, smoking and chatting, waiting to be called
for a mujra. Sultan Khan, the tabla player, was called. He came, and he
was also shocked to see that I had returned – paler, thinner, but alive.

Lal saab wants me to perform a mujra. I have forgotten all the
songs. I have lost all practice. If you support me tonight, I can make
a fresh start, I confided in Sultan Khan.

Arre arre, he said. I am with you.

I did not have a harmonium, or tabla, not even a pair of
ghungroos. How were we going to manage it?

Sultan Khan arranged for the musicians.

Do you remember the song you sang?

Yes, the popular ones that were easy to recollect like 'Ramaiyya
vastavaiyya'.

Rasta wahi aur musafir wahi
Ek tara na jaane kahan chhup gaya.

I sang the lyrics in a nervous, weak voice, trying to find my sur.

Duniya wahi duniyawale wahi
Koi kya jaane kis ka jahaan lut gaya.

By this time, my voice was turning into a pathetic wail. I was going to break down at any moment.

Meri aankhon mein rahe kaun jo tujh se kahe
Maine dil tujh ko diya haan ramaiyya vastavaiyya.

Tears were flowing down my cheeks. Lal saab tried to remain cheerful. He smiled, giving me the strength to return to myself.

'*Ramaiyya vastavaiyya*' is a beautiful anthem of the poor. It makes us weep and smile at the same time. It has such a lilting rhythm that no eye can remain dry and no heart can be empty at the end of it. I was feeling all the despair and all the hope that the melody wove. Shailendra ka likha, Shankar–Jaikishan ka sangeet aur Lata–Rafi ka gaaya. Written by Shailendra, composed by Shankar–Jaikishan and sung by Lata–Rafi. I had heard a story that the lyricist Shailendra was passing an under-construction building when he heard the labourers lifting bricks and sand bags sing the words '*Ramaiyya vastavaiyya*'. It is an invocation to Lord Ram to be present in our hardship, just like when we say Jai Shree Ram when lifting a heavy weight, as if we are picking a boulder to drop into the ocean to help build a road for him to walk towards Lanka. Is not all work God's will?

Around ten that night, Lal saab and Pandeyji left. The kotha had heard the sounds of a new arrival. From my room, my warbling voice rose up into the air like a night bird seeking its nest. Lal saab gave me a hundred and fifty rupees for my performance. It was a lot of money for a night.

While leaving, Lal saab said, Rekha, tomorrow is a Saturday. I do not know if I will come around. Let us see what can be done on Monday, all right?

Accha, I said.

You have just arrived and you have started already, said Inder bhaiya.

His daughter, Munni, who was a beautiful woman, was startled at my success on my first night. She looked at me, cross-eyed. Jalne ki boo aa rahi thi. I could smell her burn.

How will you sleep tonight? Inder bhaiya asked.

Peacefully, I said.

At eleven, I shut the two-panelled door of my room. I bolted them both for safety.

I ate the rasgulla, the singara. Drank water from the surahi, earthen pot. I had been performing on an empty stomach. I slept, content, thanking Kali Ma for her wonders.

The next morning, around eleven, a man carrying a big envelope came looking for me.

Who is Rekha? he asked in a loud, stern voice.

I got scared and locked myself in my room. I thought someone had snitched on me to Pushpa and sent a goon to evict me.

What is the matter? Inder bhaiya asked the stranger.

I have a lifafa, envelope, for her, he said.

Aye, maudi, Inder bhaiya called out for me in his rural bedia dialect. Je aadmi tohe dhundh ro. Listen girl, this man is looking for you.

From his tone I could gather that there was nothing to fear.

I stepped out and the man said as he handed me the envelope, Lal saab has sent this for you.

I breathed a sigh of relief and thanked him. I went back to my room and opened it. I was surprised to see what it contained.

One thousand rupees!

I was shocked. Should I laugh? Should I cry? I wanted to do both. 'Ramaiyya vastavaiyya,' my heart was singing.

I did not want to gloat. Quickly, I changed into my mother's saree and went to the sutapatti bylane in Bada Bazaar.

I ordered a gaddi, bolsters, bedsheets and lots of other household items. I indulged in two sixteen-rupee sarees. They were called the Bijli saree in those days – one in shimmering red sequins and another in deep sea blue.

I want all this delivered by this evening, I said to the shopkeeper.

I went to Bow Bazaar, and bought make-up and a mirror. I had not seen myself properly in a mirror in days, even months. Again, I had spent all the money to furnish the room.

In the evening, Lal saab called on the telephone in Inder bhaiya's room.

Rekha, I sent some cash for you; get a few things for yourself, he said.

Main le aayi, I said. I've got them. I laughed and thanked him. I will never forget his generosity.

Lal saab changed his mind and arrived the same evening after I had bought the gaddi and pillows. He was with Pandeyji and another friend, Vinit.

Looks much better, he said. Have you cooked something?

I had no time to, I said. I order from Warsi restaurant across the street, where the ustads sit.

Bulao ustadon ko, he said. Call the ustads.

Sultan Khan came with the other musicians. I sang and earned a total of three hundred rupees that night.

Later, I told the ustads, Look, I cannot pay you tonight. I have to pay my first month's rent with this earning. Can you wait till another mujra?

Sure, they said. Sultan Khan left for Kankurganchi, where he lived.

On his way out, Lal saab slipped another one hundred rupees into my hand. Now I had the exact amount for the rent.

That night, it was too late to procure any food from outside, so I slept after drinking a few glasses of water. I was happy. Hunger was keeping me alive.

Sunday morning I gave Inder bhaiya four hundred rupees for the rent. I was left with nothing. Surprisingly, Sultan Khan came to see me in the morning.

Have you eaten anything, baccha? he asked. What would you like to eat?

Dal tadka and roti, I said.

He pulled out twenty rupees from his kurta. He gave it to me. I sent Inder bhaiya's servant, Ramu, to Warsi. Khan saab and I shared the meal. I saved some for dinner.

Now, since it was a Sunday and Munni was the most famous baiji in the kotha, people came for her. A crowd gathered at her door. People queued up to get in for a mujra session. No one came to my door. Why would they? Lal saab was a loyal customer from my previous kotha. No one knew me here yet. The dalals, pimps, had, of course, heard that I had arrived. They tried to persuade the crowd to move to my room.

Bajrang, a stringy dalal with a weak, thin voice, got a Marwari customer. A fat man in a safari suit. He took one look at me and said, Yeh chhori gaana gayegi? This girl will sing? Kamzor lagti hai. She is so frail.

Aap baith ke toh dekhiye, suniye toh sahi, said Bajrang. Why don't you sit and watch, hear her sing?

It was my first dance performance. I had lost practice. I did not know which song to dance to. An ustad suggested 'Kajra mohabbat wala'.

Haan, dikhao, show, the fat Marwari said.

I hummed the tune and started moving my ghungrooed feet on the beats. I tapped as the ustad beat the tabla.

'Kajra mohabbat wala, ankhiyon mein aisa daala, kajre ne le li meri jaan.'

I sang nervously because I was sure he would not like it, no matter how hard I tried. The Marwari, though, was easy to please. His eyes were on my hips. All I had to do was shake and twirl and sing, 'Haye re main tere qurbaan', and he was floored.

Duniya hai mere peechhe
Lekin main tere peechhe.

I used the lyrics to tap one foot and undulate the other hip, synchronizing it with the beats on the tabla.

> *Apna bana le meri jaan*
> *Haye re main tere qurbaan.*

I did the twirl again.

> *Haye re main tere qurbaan!*

The Marwari must have felt he was the most desirable man in the room.

He gave me five hundred rupees for my performance. That looked like another month's rent was covered. After distributing it amongst the ustads, I had around three hundred rupees left with me this time. It had been a good Sunday night.

By Monday morning, I has hired a servant boy, Ismail. Twenty rupees a month with tips extra. The room had a loft area, where the kitchen was set up. Money was spent on mutton – twelve rupees a kilo – and gulab swaroop fragrant rice at twelve rupees a kilo. Ismail was a very good boy. He was useful in fetching alcohol for the customers, the ustads, you name it; he worked like a bee, quick on his heels for any errand in the hope of earning tips. I did not have to worry about cooking and cleaning.

Ab ittefaq se mera dhanda itna chala, itna chala, Munni bai ka ho gaya thapp! My business picked up and Munni's went phuuss, kaput!

Munni soon became jealous of my success. Stories began to float around that I was of loose character. That I was favouring the men and showering them with special attention. That I was a sleazy performer. She came from lineage. I was a hillbilly who got plain lucky. Pushpa got word of my rising fame. She waited for a month or so to see if I was a fluke, a candle that would soon snuff itself out in the wind. When that did not happen, I started receiving word through the ustads that she wanted to meet me. She wanted me to return. She said my husband was waiting for me. That my in-laws were missing me. I said no. I was never going to return to them. I said I would never step into their kotha.

Pushpa sent Ramlal, my husband, to stalk me. There was a soodi khana, liquor den, across the balcony. He began to visit it every night. He would stand below the balcony and simply look at me. He never said anything. He just stood there, waiting for me to call him upstairs. After many such nights, I decided to call him up to ask him why he was hanging around.

Aye, Ramlal, why do you come here? I asked.

To see you, he said.

Accha, I said. What do you see in me?

I want to live with you, he said. Please let me stay here with you.

Oh, so you want to be my bhadwa, pimp? I said. You want me to earn and feed you?

His gall to even suggest that we could be together again enraged me.

Do you think I am like Saroj, bhaadkhau, pimp?

Saroj was a tawaif. She was Inder bhaiya's wife. She used to earn; he used to manage her funds.

You want us to be like Inder–Saroj? I said.

Ramlal was quiet. He had never seen me like this. I did not fear him. I did not cower down. I was ready to fight him.

Chal bhaag yahan se, I said. Get out of here. I slapped him. My hand did not shake. My heart beat noisily in my chest.

Ek laat maarungi teri gaand pe, seedha ho jayega! I will kick you so hard in your ass that you will fall in line, I said.

I had mastered the language of the kotha. I had to speak it if required. Such people deserved no less.

Bhaag yahan se! I screamed.

He left. But that did not stop him from reappearing below the balcony the very next night. Pushpa's new girl, Chitra, did not turn

out to be the cash cow they were hoping for. Pushpa was desperate
to see me, but did not have the courage to face my wrath this time.
She realized that Chitra, despite her good looks, did not have the
same naseeb as me. She began admitting as much and spreading the
good word in the hope that I would melt. I was not that easy to
please, though. My heart had seen very little kindness in people so
far. I understood cunning better than love. I sent back a strong word.
I said, If you guys do not stop harassing me, I will report you to the
Lal Bazaar police station. I was bluffing, but I hoped they would get
the message loud and clear.

I sent a warning to Pushpa: Tell this Ramlal to disappear from
here. They did not heed my word. There was a wooden furniture
store in the area, where a man named Bhagwan dada used to work
as a carpenter. He was a Bengali man known to have a short temper
and a soft spot for women in distress. I went to him and played the
helpless-woman card. I told him everything sacchi-sacchi, truthfully,
in good faith. I said I was a single girl and that they had done so
many horrible things to me in the past. He heard me out.

Where does he stand? he asked.

I showed him the spot where Ramlal would appear later that
evening.

Bhagwan dada went to a soodi khana, drank to his heart's
content and came to the spot in time to find Ramlal lurking below
the balcony.

Teri maa ka, madarchod, teri behen ka, behenchod! You mother-
sister fucker! Dada shouted and pounded him with blows. Ladki ko
pareshan karega, haan! You think you can harass the girl?

Ramlal got a good thrashing. I made sure all the girls in the
kotha watched from the balcony. Ramlal saw us lined up like mute
spectators, enjoying the show. If we had been singing, we would have
sung a great, anthemic song to his beating. Silently, we watched him
as if we were all in this together. It was a show of solidarity. The girls

looked down on him as my assertion of power and identity. Both ways, I had nothing to lose, but I could cement my status in the kotha. No one was going to mess with me now.

Dada looked up and yelled, Rekha didi, aap aaram se rahiye; yahan ab sala koi bhatkega nahi. Iss madarchod ko hum dekh lenge. Sister, you stay put; no scoundrel will stray here any more. I will take care of this motherfucker.

Everyone heard my name, the respect that a goon gave me by calling me his didi, sister. Dada kicked him. Ramlal lay on the ground, whimpering and crying for mercy. I did not feel a thing for that wuss of a man. Rekha, Rekha, Rekha – my name began to echo in the kotha. I was making a lot of money every night. Was this not why I was there? The chant of my name on everyone's lips was currency of my confidence and popularity. A year went by. I had settled in comfortably. I sent a telegram to my mother. Before I had left Poona, I had found the local post office, got her address down and noted her name as Gulshan devi. Subsequently I began sending her money orders. Ekyasi number used to be an empty kotha before I came. Afterwards, all the rooms got filled up because of me. As I got famous, word also spread that despite the fame, I had no background, no lineage, no class and no culture. I am not denying that all of this is true, but one can cultivate it, right?

Meena, Munni, Lata, Sharda – all these girls knew how to read books. In the evening, after they had dolled up, they would sit in their rooms with an upanyas, a novel, or a book of Hindi-film-song lyrics. I yearned to be like them. Literate. They used to read the Hindi novels of Ved Prakash and Gulshan Nanda, Om Prakash, Surenda Mohan Pathak and Anil Mohan. These books had titillating covers in bright colours. Kahani thodi *open* hoti thi. They always featured a woman in trouble or being rescued by a man. Such themes fascinated me. I wanted to know what lay beyond the bold covers. I learnt to read all of them later. I read a lot of books, so much so that I had my own library at one point in time. Later, I discarded the books in raddi, scrap. What would I achieve by hoarding so many books when we lived in such cramped rooms?

Baharhaal, anyway, I met a Bihari masterji, Shiv Shankar. He was quite handsome. He used to wear a white dhoti–kurta. He used to teach some girls how to read and write in Hindi at home for a small fee of twenty rupees a month. I was keen on learning to read more than writing, so when he came in the evening to teach I would insist that he show me how to read first. When it was time for the writing exercise, an hour would pass as I would write glacially. A party would arrive by then. I would have to shut the notebooks and turn the classroom into a mujra hall.

One day, it so happened that I was sitting in one corner of my room, practising how to write A Aa E Ee O Oo, on my own. Masterji was absent that day. I was reading the letters aloud as I wrote them. A gentleman was crossing my room to use the toilet when he heard me. He peeped in through the window and watched me. He then walked over to the door and knocked.

Kaun? Who? I shouted.

Mohtarma, kya hum andar aa sakte hain? Madam, may I come in?

I felt a current bolt up my spine. I stood up and walked towards the door. No one had ever called me a mohtarma. Mohtarma. A respectable woman.

Shekhar was standing at my door. He was Munni's patron. I knew of him. He was in his early fifties, maybe. Not old, but not young either, although strident in his voice. He was dressed in fine fabric, with slicked-back hair and an air of royalty that other patrons did not have. He had never come to my room before. He was from Kanpur. He was said to be from a rich family. He was a tameezdaar aadmi. A man of impeccable good manners.

Aiye, come in, I said.

I was wearing an aasmaani-coloured, sky-blue, Banarasi silk saree that Lal saab had gifted me. I had worn make-up and mogra flowers in my hair.

Kya main idhar baith sakta hoon? May I sit here? he asked.

Baithiye, sit, I said.

I did not have the same manners as him. My tone was neutral.

Kya kar rahi hain aap? What are you doing? he asked.

I was holding a black slate and chalk in my hands.

Padh rahi hoon, I am studying, I said.

Kya main dekh sakta hoon? May I see?

I gave him the slate. He looked at my crooked handwriting and smiled.

Acchi baat, nice, he said. Toh aap padhti bhi hain. So you study as well.

Haan, yes, I said.

Toh aap gaati aur raqs bhi karti hain, ya sirf unme se ek? So do you sing and dance, or do you just do one of those things? he asked.

Dono, both, I said.

Kya aap mere liye kuch pesh karengi? Will you please sing and dance for me? he asked politely.

Nahi, no, I said. Aap Munni ke raees hain; aap ki jagah wahan hai. Mere yahan kuch doosre raees aane wale hain. You are Munni's patron, that is where you belong. My party will be here soon.

Kyon? Why? he asked. Kya aap ko lagta hai hum aap ke fann ki qadr nahi karenge? Do you think I will not respect your art?

Haye haye, I thought. What exquisite Urdu. So much adab. Such politeness. It was uprooting my loyalty to my regular patrons.

Nahi, no, it is not that, I said. Aaj time nahi hai. I do not have time today.

Ho sakey toh time nikaal lijiye mere liye. Please make some time for me today, he said.

He took out fifty rupees from his wallet and placed it in my hand.

Maaf kijiyega, aap ka waqt zayar kiya humne. Sorry, I wasted your time, he said. Please accept this token as my apology.

Before I could say a word, he left. He had paid for a mujra session without hearing a tune.

He went back to Munni's room and probably nursed his hurt with a drink. Lal saab, my regular patron, soon arrived with his cronies. My mujra began. It went on almost till midnight.

After they left, I was undressing in my room when I heard a knock. Shekhar was back.

Kya aap masruuf hain? Are you still busy? he asked.

Ji, yes, I said.

I did not want to encourage him and earn Munni's ire.

Kya main kal aa sakta hoon? Can I come tomorrow? he asked. Aap mere liye kuch pesh karengi? Will you please perform for me?

He took out another fifty-rupee note and placed it in my hand.

Advance, he said.

I smiled and said, Theek hai. All right.

When he arrived the next day, he went straight to Munni's room first and then excused himself. I saw him and hid from his view. After some time, he arrived at my door.

Look, I said. You are sitting there. If you want me to perform for you, Munni will have to invite me to her room and I will entertain you there.

Oh, is that the rivaaj, system, of the kotha? he asked.

Yes, I said. I can only come there as a one-time guest performer, so that I do not poach her patron. It is an understood practice between us girls.

Tell the dalal to fetch me, I said.

He went to Inder bhaiya.

Please call the mohtarma who lives in the middle room, he said.

Inder bhaiya did not want to call me.

Munni is a better dancer, he said to Shekhar.

Shekhar insisted on me.

O, Rekha maudi, o maudi, tohe bula rahe. Inder bhaiya defeatedly came for me.

Is your party calling me for a mujra? I asked.

Haan, he said.

I called the ustads. We went to Munni's room. Munni was a star singer. Star dancer. She could play the veena, the sitar. She was beautiful. I was entering her chamber. I knew I was breaking some unspoken code of sisterhood.

Salaam, I said to all of them.

I sang a few ghazals. And a few tawaif songs like '*Main tawaif hoon mujra karungi*'. No great shakes. No one was impressed. How could they be? Munni was the queen of the kotha.

Could you please also show us a dance? Shekhar requested.

I whispered to the ustads to set up the melody for a qawwali.

I did the intro claps to the tune of the tabla and the harmonium, following it up with a few quick spins and some rehearsed steps involving my hips matching rhythm with the beats.

I stopped and sang the sher.

Raaz ki baat hain mehfil mein kahein ya naa kahein
Bas gaya hain koyi iss dil mein kahein ya naa kahein.

After quoting the couplet as I twirled and sang the first line of the song '*Nigahe milane ko jee chahata hai*', I noticed Shekhar had removed the clip of a bundle of one rupee notes and had spread all of them at my feet.

Yeh kya kar rahein hain aap? I asked. What are you doing? The music stopped.

Maybe he was used to his royal pedigree.

Kya hua, kya aap khush nahi hain? he asked. What happened, are you not happy?

Dekhiye, I said. Sure, I dance for the money. I cannot dance on it.

He understood it was disrespectful to ask a girl to dance on the money we called Goddess Lakshmi.

He collected the notes and gave them to me.

Sorry, he said.

I took the bundle from him with respect. Kissed the notes with my eyes, handed them to the ustad and continued the dance from where I had left off, taking it from the second line.

Dil-o-jan lutane ko jee chahata hai.

Shekhar was besotted. He left for Kanpur the next day. When he returned after a week, he gifted me a VIP make-up box.

Yeh aap ke liye hai, mohtarma, he said. This is for you, my lady.

Uff, his unimpeachable manners.

In those days, I did not have a vanity case. Munni had one. Only the well-to-do girls had a case. When I opened it, I saw a gorgeous saree – as black as night with a gold patta – inside it. I still have it in an almirah somewhere. Shekhar soon started taking me out for fancy dinners. He spent a lot to groom me.

Kamandal aapa, a tawaif, who was fading, used to live in Chowdhury ki baari. She used to go to the Ajmer dargah.

Once, she gave me the tabaruk (blessed holy offering) and said, Yeh sirf naseeb walo ko milta hai. Only the very fortunate get this.

She said it with such arrogance and disdain that I felt small. Or that was her intention. She always thought no end of herself.

I took the tabaruk and joked, Naseeb ka kya hai, I will also go. I was adamant to make my own destiny as I had learnt to do when I broke free of Pushpa's stranglehold.

Kamandal aapa made a face and left. After a few months, I dreamt of a dargah. I did not give it much thought. Another few months later, I had the same dream. I began wondering why I kept seeing this dargah. I told Shekhar about my recurring dream.

I want to go to Ajmer, I said.

I broke my gulak. I had saved some money in it. It was not enough, but I could manage if I tried. This new obsession of going to Ajmer was consuming me.

Shekhar returned to Kanpur. He arranged for a railway ticket to Delhi, via Kanpur. At the Kanpur station, when the train halted, he came to see me. He garlanded me with marigold and rose flowers, and gave me some money. He was more enthused about my trip than I was. I was going because the thought of going to Ajmer was enough. It was an act of defiance.

What mannat will you ask for? he asked.

Nothing, I said. I just want to see it.

In Delhi, there was an ustad who came to receive me at the station. His name was Ejaaz Khan. He used to play the tabla for me when he used to come to Calcutta. He showed me the Nizamuddin Auliya dargah, the Chiragh Dehlvi dargah and some others. We visited G.B. Road and met some bais. The next day he put me on an evening train to Ajmer.

You will reach Ajmer by dawn, he said.

The train was so slow; it was close to evening when we finally reached within half a kilometre of the main station. People started deboarding. I also got restless, so I got down. I was carrying only a handbag. We walked like pilgrims, following the train tracks.

The sun had set by the time I got out of the station. I told a rickshaw-wala to take me to the Ajmer dargah. He said it was evening. I should freshen up before going there. He took me to a hotel across from the railway station called Hotel Sartaj.

I went in and asked for a room. The owner, a sardarji, Narender Singh, looked at me carefully and asked if I was alone.

Yes, I said.

What have you come for? he asked.

I told him I was from Calcutta. I had come to see the dargah. It was my first visit.

He gave me a room without registering my name and address in the logbook.

I was hungry, so I asked for a cup of tea to be sent to my room. The tea arrived. I was ready to leave for the dargah. I went back to the sardarji and told him to fetch a vehicle for me to visit the dargah.

It is late night, why do you want to go now? he asked.

I insisted. He called his servant, Bundu.

Look, take the memsahib to the dargah in a tanga, horse-drawn carriage, and make sure you wait till she gets out. Do not return without her, he instructed Bundu.

The sardarji had understood that I was alone and lost.

Bundu took me to the Buland Darwaza. I purchased a tokri of rose petals and walked in. Before I could reach the maqbara of Khwaja Moinuddin Chishti, I tripped and fell. When I looked up, I could see the brightly lit marble dome, the white entrance gate with gold lettering. I realized this was exactly the manzar I had seen in my dreams.

I went in and kissed the cloth on the tomb. I prayed, but did not ask for any mannat.

The next morning, the kind sardarji arranged a khadim saab, a servant of god, to show me the entire dargah. After a few days I returned and offered the tabaruk to Kamandal.

Apne naseeb se layi hoon, see what my destiny got me, I said to her.

She did not know how to react. Going to Ajmer prepared me to travel alone. I began travelling frequently – I went to Pushkar and many other religious sites. I began taking other bais along with me after a few years: Mallika aapa, Meena, Geeta. Many years later, when Kamandal was old, she asked me to take her to Ajmer. Naseeb naseeb ki baat hai! It's a matter of one's destiny!

Once, I told Shekhar I had to go to Ahmedabad for a relative's wedding. He said to come along with him to Delhi. He would go to Kanpur from there; I could go to Ahmedabad. We travelled together to Delhi. When we arrived, he took me to the airport. It was the first time I had seen an airplane. He looked at his watch and said, You will reach Ahmedabad in two hours. Here is your ticket.

I will not go in, I said.

I was scared of walking into such a huge place alone. I was too young to be on my own.

Do not worry, he said. You will go. I know it.

Please send me by train, I begged him.

No, he said, you will go by plane.

He saw that I was petrified.

Okay, let us have a cup of coffee first, he said.

We sat in a café and sipped on coffee. Shekhar looked around and spotted a sardarji sitting alone. He went and spoke to the man. A sardar is always around when you need help. Kamaal ki baat hai. It's amazing.

Sir, he asked, are you going to Ahmedabad?

Yes, the man said.

You see, he said, this young lady is also going to Ahmedabad. She is all alone and it is her first time on a plane. Could you please guide her through the security and till the plane lands in Ahmedabad? She will find her way from the airport. The sardarji looked at me and did not suspect anything strange. I did look like a bundle of nerves.

Okay, he said.

Shekhar soon said bye to me and left. I followed the sardarji wherever he went, almost going into the men's loo once. I waited outside like his doting wife. He helped me on the bus to the plane. I did not know how to wear the seatbelt. An air hostess helped me at the window seat I was allotted.

Life gives you a window seat to belong in the world when you feel lost. I looked out of the window, trying to breathe calmly through my fears. I was floating in the clouds, looking at the sun. The world was one with me, filling my lungs with confidence. At the Ahmedabad airport, I took an auto and went to see my relatives. Shekhar had made me realize how self-reliant I could be. I was always headstrong, but he made me fearless.

Shekhar took me to Lucknow many times. I visited a lot of dargahs. He once put me in a first-class cabin meant for ministers while travelling back from Lucknow to Calcutta. Everything was white inside – white bedsheets, white pillows, white curtains, a white washbasin, white seats – all so stark and clean and smelling like white jasmine flowers. He introduced me to so much elegance that I always felt special, despite my ordinariness. He never gave me money – I mean, not a lot. He gave me a lot of respect. That meant more to me as a young woman who had not yet understood the value of money. If one is given respect in their youth, one begins to build character, rather than chase money. In our profession, especially, earning respect before money gives us a sense of integrity that spreads far and wide, bringing money wherever we go.

Shekhar made me look at myself with dignity. To hold my head up and walk, to not look at my clothes, to not be conscious of my aukaat, but be firm in shaping my destiny. We went to Kashmir. I combed my hair in a shikara on Dal Lake, the sun flushing my cheeks. I rode a horse in Pahalgam. Ate apples and cashews in the snow. It was all like a dream with him around.

Shekhar also took me to Kathmandu, which I had only seen in the film *Hare Rama Hare Krishna*. I was always ready to travel because I wanted to visit temples and dargahs. I liked going to religious places. It offers solace to the lost. I wanted to see the Pashupatinath temple.

We stayed in a nice hotel. I liked the mornings in Nepal. The air was so fresh. I felt so alive there. Shekhar was an old man compared to me, but he was such a gentleman that I did not mind spending time with him. Obviously, people stared at us when we went out together, but we were not in love or married. He knew how to maintain his dignity in public. He never treated me badly. He gifted me lots of clothes and took care of all my expenses. We went to the casino in a hotel. A driver used to come to pick us up for sightseeing in the morning. The driver used to give me a rose every morning. The people were so nice to me, or maybe it was just them treating me like a tourist.

On our Nepal trip, a friend of Shekhar, Shakir, had come with us. He was staying in another room. Shakir used to call me Rekh. One day he asked me, Rekh, do you have a hundred and fifty rupees with you?

Yes, I said, quickly giving it to him from my purse.

He went out and returned to the hotel with a green bottle of champagne. None of us had ever seen or tasted it before.

Hold two glasses while I open the bottle, he said.

I stood in front of him, following his instructions and swaying with the bottle as he struggled to open it. He did not know how to uncork it.

Hold this, I said, handing him the glasses. Let me try.

I had an idea. I pulled out a hairpin from my bun, pricked the cork and yanked it out. The cork flew across the room, and so did the champagne, shooting out like an arrow. I stumbled in shock, trying to hold on to the bottle. Shakir danced around me and managed to get some of the foamy liquid in the glasses.

What is this? I asked him.

Gud ka kaada, he said. Jaggery juice. Drink it.

We laughed and drank the champagne. It tasted like a sweet peach. I enjoyed shopping a lot in Kathmandu. The gold had a pure yellow lustre, different from that in Calcutta. I purchased some jewellery. I bought a gold pen for my young brother, Dasrath. We travelled back across Patna to Calcutta.

Even in Calcutta, Shekhar took me to several concerts. Once, at Kala Mandir, my favourite qawwals, the Sabri brothers, were performing. There was such a huge crowd. I felt so small walking in. Shekhar and I were sitting in the front row. How he got those tickets was no surprise to me, but finding myself right in front of the artistes made me more nervous than excited. They performed '*Tajdar-e-Haram*', '*Bhar do jholi meri ya Muhammad*', '*Aaye hai tere dar pe toh kuch le ke jayenge*'. At one point, Shekhar gave me a hundred-rupee note, inspired by the lyrics of that qawwali.

Go and give it to them, he said.

No, no, I said, I cannot. I was too shy in public to do such elitist things.

Oh ho, just go now, I know how much you like them, he said.

I walked in front and presented the ustads with a hundred-and-one-rupee token. The one rupee I added as shagun, good luck. It is funny when I think of it now. The roles had reversed. I was the raees, not the performer. I was giving away money. Later, the qawwals came to Husn Bano's kotha in Bandook Gully. Maqbool Ahmed Sabri even did a nikah with Husn Bano. The brothers came a few times to jam with the mirasis, the ustads. Many years later, when we met again, Maqbool looked like a deranged man with long, unkempt hair and the magic was missing in his voice. I used to be star-struck before, but now I was familiar with him, so I could tell him the truth.

Arre, aap aise ho gaye, kya hua? Oh, you look worn out, what happened? I asked in shock.

He smiled and tried to avoid answering my question. After all, he was ordinary like me when not on stage. After the success comes the decline. His careless appearance was a reminder that I could not let myself go when I got there.

It was around this time that I also went to see the Taj Mahal. When I had seen it with Ramlal's family, it was just an edifice that stood in the background of our ordinary lives. That changed when I went there the second time. I could see it with new eyes.

Meena, Pushpa and some other bednis who lived in Agra came with me. A tour guide explained to us the significance of the mausoleum. We listened without feeling. What did we know of love? We just giggled, frolicked and pirouetted like some heroines who were lucky to do so in films. We did our own small performance, thinking of Bina Rai in the song 'Jo wada kiya woh nibhana padega' in the film Taj Mahal.

In my second year in ekyasi number, I was on an equal footing with, or you could even say more than, Munni. What I did not achieve in singing, I doubled by dancing. When we are dancing and singing, the ustads pitch in with a jugalbandi on the instruments and the patrons are transfixed by the actions. The dance compensates for the lack of voice, but, together with the inspired act by the ustads, it is a performance of such vigour and energy that it impresses the excited patrons as a complete act.

As I grew more popular, I called my mother and Shanna to live with me. I sent a telegram.

Ma, immediately chali aao, I told the postman.

I had not studied English yet. I used to listen attentively to the patrons, and sometimes, I would use their English words, which I assumed acquired urgency when added to Hindi. 'Immediately' sounded like a word that travelled faster. Jaldi, jaldi, the patrons would add immediately. My mix of the two languages was a sign of my enthusiasm for an education. The postman used to write my messages jaldi jaldi. It used to cost more than writing a letter, but it was quick. Who had the patience to write a letter? Despite masterji's lessons, I hadn't learnt to write very well. I thought Shanna should learn first and then she could teach me to write. When my mother arrived, her straight face concealed her emotions. I think she had prepared for the worst. She did not know what the life of a naachnewali looked like. I doubt if she had ever seen a film about tawaifs. She must have heard of girls dancing in tents, but would never have imagined her own daughter doing it. She was quiet. She did not mention her famous line about naseeb. Seeing that it was nowhere near as seedy as one would imagine, she warmed up to my life. It was her first visit to the city. The fact that I gave her ten thousand rupees immediately for the marriage of my sister Rohini could have also been the reason for her warming up. On weekends, I would take them to the market and buy haldi, mehndi, clothes, jewellery, utensils – all the stuff she would need for the ceremony. Suddenly, I had become the eldest daughter of the family. Shanna did not understand the kotha at first. It was a fort for her. No open sky or green fields. She kept to herself. I asked masterji to teach her instead of me.

But how will you learn to write? he asked.

She will teach me, na, I said.

However, Shanna was not prepared for an education. She and mother spent all day with me. In the evening, when the lights came on, the two would retire upstairs in the kitchen area, sitting there till midnight for the naach-gaana to conclude. I used to tell Shanna to not drink too much water sitting upstairs. I did not want the men's eyes to fall on her if she descended the stairs to use the toilet. She was a pretty ten-year-old girl. I wanted her to study and become smarter than me. The servant boy, Ismail, would stand outside the door to serve alcohol and snacks. Since my mother and Shanna did not speak fluent Hindi and I had forgotten their dialect, we only spoke in clipped words to one another. They never questioned my profession or asked me to quit. They did not know any better. When mother left to prepare for Rohini's wedding, Shanna stayed back. We used to listen to the radio in our spare time. I always thought of the radio as a teacher. With time, I was able to distinguish between the voices of Asha, Lata, Geeta, Noor Jehan, Suraiya, Hemlata, Sudha, Vani, Mubarak Begum, Rajkumari, Shamshad Begum, Parveen, Naseem, Suman, and even Kamal Barot, whose duet with Lata – 'Hansta hua noorani chehra' – was our go-to mujra opener. It became a guessing game for me. I was not always right. But the radio announcer Ameen Sayani was always right. The radio began to bother Munni. She said it was disturbing her riyaaz. Khisyane lagi. Munni became irritable. Shekhar was also visiting me regularly, switching from Munni's room to mine.

She is competing directly with me now, Munni complained.

She did not like the sound of her own words. Munni and Inder bhaiya decided that something had to be done about me.

Inder bhaiya also started commenting about the radio. I could feel the heat being directed towards me. I became scared that they might hurt my little sister. They would taunt her if she went out to buy sweets. She was a simple girl. She did not know how to cope with brutes. She would cry. They told her that I was going to sell her in the flesh trade. She did not even understand what it meant. She used to get upset, but remained quiet about it. I had to quarrel for her safety. It began to take a toll on my mental health as well. Had I been on my own, I would have fought back tooth and nail. Shanna became my weakness. I had thought I could make her strong like me. Seeing her cry and become meek ... Poor thing! Bacchi hi thi na. She was just a child. I could not bear to see her suffer in silence. I could tell that she did not enjoy the environment. No one befriended her. She was also not the friendly kind. She seemed lost in the kotha, but was also helpless because Gullo had left her here with me, so she could only hope that her mother would return and take her away. She did not like the place or the people, but she preferred not to voice it because she understood she was there for her sister – for me. One day, I confided in Sultan Khan, the tabla player. Gingerly, I asked him if he was aware of any other kotha with vacant rooms where I could shift. People in this building were making it difficult for me to survive.

Haan, he said, there is one in Bandook Gully.

Just hearing the name of the street gave me palpitations.

Bandook Gully! I said. Baap re, there are so many famous bais there – Moni didi, Kamini didi, Sakuntala didi, Geeta didi. I do not know how it got its name Bandook Gully – literally meaning a street where guns went off – but the name alone inspired dread.

I used the suffix of endearment 'didi' out of respect for them. I had never met them. I had only heard of their fame. They were celebrated artistes. They only sang. They did not perform mujras. Their evenings were called baithaks, in which they sang classical songs, not filmy gaane. I tried to reason with him that it might not be an ideal kotha for me.

Will it not be too far from the bazaar? I asked.

If you want, I can check, he said.

I suspect he wanted to put me in a bigger pond. The fish in this pond were rotten.

He took me to Zakaria Street to meet the mutwalli Yahya saab – the trustee of the kotha that was under the Waqf Board. There was an imambara, a tomb, on the ground floor of the kotha.

It will cost you twelve thousand for the room. I will have to renovate it. This is the salaami amount. You will have ownership of the room for as long as you wish. No one will evict you – I will sign as guarantor. You will also pay a monthly rent of two hundred and fifty rupees, for which a rent bill will be issued in your name, he said.

Twelve thousand rupees, I wondered aloud.

I had just given my mother ten thousand. How was I going to produce that much cash so soon?

In how many days will the room be ready? I asked.

A month, he said.

Between Sultan Khan and me, we had two thousand rupees on us. I gave Yahya Khan the amount as an advance and returned home. I did not whisper about it to anyone, except one person.

Hey, Kali Ma, I said to the goddess in a nearby temple. Please somehow arrange the money for this. I do not have it.

It was mata's karishma, miracle, that in fifteen days I had the required amount ready. I did so many mujras that even I got tired. I gave the money to the mutwalli. He asked me to come along with him and check the kotha.

I will come when it is ready, I said. I trust that you will do a good job.

Actually, I was not prepared to go there. I was afraid that I would bump into the badi-badi gayikas, singers, and I might become self-conscious and look like an upstart in front of them. I wanted to arrive with a buzz.

Munni and Inder bhaiya, meanwhile, began doing jaadu-tona, black magic, on Shanna and me. I would find a nail hammered to the door. Ash was scattered outside my room. My radio disappeared – as if it had grown wings and flown away with a breezy melody. Clothes vanished from the balcony. Then they began to route the customers from the street towards their rooms, not allowing anyone to lurk anywhere close to my door.

Petty quarrels turned into hair-pulling competitions a few times. All the other girls stood around and watched like it was a wrestling match. One time, when I could not take it any more, I beat Saroj to a pulp. Inder bhaiya tried to intervene politely, but what else could he do? He was a bechara himself.

All the girls wanted me out. I also got aggressive because I knew I was going to leave the next month. So why not leave with a lasting impression? I made sure everyone got a taste of my temper. At some point, I think I was just thrilled at my own acts of violence. I was exacting revenge on anyone who slighted me. It was perhaps my way of getting back at everyone who had mistreated me in life before I found my voice.

Fine, I will go, I announced during one of my catfights. Your party will come looking for me. Wait and watch.

And that is exactly what happened.

When I moved into the room in Bandook Gully, I walked up a staircase, passing the rooms of the seasoned baijis. My room was on the terrace. It was newly constructed. I could see two rooms that faced each other. There was a room adjacent to mine, but it was locked.

All the bais whispered that a new tenant had come to occupy a ready-made room, one especially furnished for her. The room was spacious. It had a wooded partition wall in the middle, covering only half the length of the room. One could use the area as two separate rooms with a purdah. The room had two doors. This was good, for I could keep Shanna behind the curtain with access to another door. I had beginner's luck on the first night. Munni's party came looking for me. Everyone could hear the strains of a riotous mujra descending from the terrace. The bais were impressed and kept their distance. No one came to see me.

A long gap of dry days followed. No party showed up. Maybe the women downstairs sent them away. Maybe the parties in ekyasi number were told lies about my departure. Even Shekhar did not come to see me. I had not been able to inform him of my departure in time, because he used to live in Kanpur. Or maybe the bais had told him that I had left the city. Only much later did he come to Bandook Gully. A single bulb flickered on the terrace outside my room. It was a huge terrace, and it often felt like I was staying in an under-construction building with a room on top for a guard or labourer. Men would come up only to use the public loo at one end.

I began to feel worried. What was I going to do here? I had an unusually quiet sister for company. It was just the two of us under a vast expanse of the night sky in an isolated area of the city. I felt I had made a mistake coming here. I felt scared for our lives. If there were people downstairs, one could hear the strains of faint music. Other than that, we were disappearing into the night like the silent fading of stars. This went on for a month. Many regular patrons did not turn up to see me. Maybe they had been fed lies about my disappearance. I had not told a soul about moving here because I wanted to keep it a secret. It was not a smart move.

The bais of Bandook Gully thought I was a bedni – a renegade bedni or a bedni who was a sex worker. And they were from musical gharanas and did not mix with sex workers.

One day, Geeta didi came upstairs and asked, Are you the famous Rekha?

I do not know about that, I said, trying to deflect.

We have heard that you are a great dancer, she said.

That statement clearly divided us. The kotha in Bandook Gully housed qawwalas and classical singers. They did not dance. They looked down on it as cheap entertainment. I was going to have to prove myself worthier than that, I realized.

Can you sing a note for me? she asked.

I thought she was joking.

Not in front of you, I said.

I was nervous. I tried to smile.

I am serious, she said.

Not a muscle moved in her face.

If I refuse now, I will be crushed, I thought.

Jisse tu qubool kar le woh adaa kahan se laoon,
Tere dil ko jo lubhaa le vo sadaa kahaan se laoon.

I sang only the first two lines of the hit song, ending it with a repeat of the first, '*Jisse tu qubool kar le*' as a plangent closure.

She smiled. She probably realized that I was no competition. The next day, she sent her ustadji, Amir bhai, to train me in music. He said he could trace his own musical lineage to the Kirana gharana. Everyone here was from some gharana or the other. I was only a newcomer in a new ghar and intended to make that my own gharana. Soon the queue outside Geeta's door was dispersed. She started sending a few of her parties to me. It was the beginning of a long and beautiful friendship with the supremely talented women in the kotha. They knew I was not going to snatch away their patrons, who were serious listeners of classical music.

If I give you a few, mere kam nahi ho jayenge, it won't lessen my work, Geeta said.

She had a generous heart. The serious, mature listeners gathered downstairs. The excited young men marched up to the terrace to my room.

Three months after my arrival, Mallika Nigar, a qawwala who had a room on the terrace, returned from Bombay. She had been a great beauty in her youth, known for her sharp features, long, lustrous, straight hair and fair skin. She had a full-throated voice and had dabbled as an extra in films as well. She claimed that she was the mistress of some small-time filmmaker, but things had soured between them. It had turned her into a chronic alcoholic. I have always been friendly with the elderly. And for some strange reason, they, too, take a strong liking to me immediately. Mallika aapa and I struck up a friendship within a few days of her return.

Aap ke baal bahut khubsoorat hain, aapa, I said. You have beautiful hair. I had frizzy hair.

She laughed and hugged me. She was so warm. She was back to re-establish herself, but who was going to come watch an aged has-been? I think she was aware of that, so she hung around my room all the time, in the hope that my patrons would ask her to sing. I was also not inconsiderate. When I had a surfeit of customers, I used to send the men to her room and ask them to treat it like a waiting room. Mallika had hung glossy portraits of her in filmy poses on her walls. They were suspended in such a way that her bosom drooped like fruits from a bough. Which man would not like to wait in such a museum of tits! This arrangement suited Mallika aapa. She served them snacks and drinks, and tried to keep them engaged till I was ready for the mujra. Occasionally, I would intersperse my performance with her qawwali as fillers. Some patrons did not mind. She was fantastic, but how could an artiste survive the lure of cheap imitation? She was an original. I was only mimicking Hindi-film heroines. Young patrons loved that sort of thing – the idea of possessing an unattainable screen goddess in the artless but sincere imitation by a local tawaif. Mallika aapa did not mind that she did not get as much attention or applause as she deserved. She was past her prime and she understood that very well. She was able to make a quick buck and that was what mattered. When she got drunk, she would recount tales about her struggle in Hindi films. Once, when she got a bit role as a chorus girl in *Chaudhvin Ka Chand*, she envied the attention Waheeda Rehman got. She joked that she should have been the heroine, not Waheeda. Mallika aapa would often recount this story while chugging her drink and chuckled that if she were the heroine, the film would have been fittingly named 'Chaudhvin Ki Raand'!

Next up was my acquaintance, Meena, whom I knew from my days in ekyasi number, who came to live next to my room. She was a bedni. She took up Kamandal aapa's room on rent. Kamandal aapa had shifted to another kotha long ago. In ekyasi, Meena and I were neighbours, but she was the backbiting type. She used to be nice to my face but bitch about me to the landlord, Inder bhaiya. I did not mind it so much because most of the girls were like that, especially since they came from a long-established tradition where the bedni community supplied girls to the tawaif culture. Since I was an outsider, it was natural for them to begrudge my successes. I welcomed her to Bandook Gully quite cordially.

Why did you leave from ekyasi? I asked Meena.

We had a fight with the landlord, she said.

I did not say much. The same landlord whom she used to gossip about me to. Khair, anyway, I thought.

Meena was very fashionable. She looked like Padma Khanna, but wanted to imitate Jaya Prada. She colour-coordinated all her outfits, down to her bindi, lipstick and chutila, the decorative braid tassel, which all had the same shade. Everything had to match, or she would not wear it. She also made sure she never repeated her sarees. She was secretly jealous of my dhanda, but tried to keep it friendly. She used to think she could sing, dance and had more grace than me. I was slightly ujjad – rustic. I did not have her finesse; her refinement was all the more apparent in her snobbish attitude towards me. But it did not affect me because her patrons would leave her and come to me. That used to piss her off. She used to dance on a thali – that was her thing – but even I had my own acrobatic skill in dance. So sometimes, while dancing, I would turn my back to the audience and bend over on my back, like in a chakrasana pose, but without my hands touching the ground. I would pick a currency note from a patron's hand with my mouth. This used to turn on a lot of men, thinking about my flexibility.

I think it was around this time that I got one of the biggest jolts in my life. It is good in way that all bad things happened to me so early in life – so that there were no surprises left for later. I was too young myself when Laccha, my youngest sister, was born in our house in Poona. She was fondly called Laccha. My father, the drunkard, was quite capable of selling his daughter for a bottle of liquor. He met a bedni woman, who told him she was going to

Calcutta. He told her to take Laccha with her and bring her to my kotha. She gave him some money for liquor, so he trusted her to be a good woman. She took Laccha to Agra and from there they came to Calcutta. The bedni took my sister to another kotha, where her sister, Kamlesh, used to live.

I received a telegram from Poona asking if Laccha was keeping well with me. It was from my mother. I was surprised. When did Laccha arrive here? I had not seen her in many years; I myself had left home when I was married as a child and sent to Agra. Was the same story repeating itself with my baby sister? How could this happen? I was not going to allow it. A chacha, uncle, wrote a letter to me, saying Laccha had been taken away by a bedni. I knew most of the bednis in Bow Bazaar. I immediately started looking in every kotha in the area. It was not that difficult to find her because the bednis would not go beyond Bow Bazaar. I found out from a friend that a new girl had arrived in the building next to Sattawandi. I went to Kamlesh's house.

Where is my sister? I asked her. Bring her to me.

Kamlesh and her sister said they had paid for her, and she no longer belonged to me. They had hidden her away.

Who did you give money to? I asked.

To your father, Kamlesh said.

My father? My father is a drunkard. How can he have a say in any matter? In my house, the women make all the decisions, I said.

They would not listen to me. They started arguing and quarrelling with me.

Bring her right now, or I will walk across the street to the Lal Bazaar police station and bring the police with me, I said. I will make sure all of you are in handcuffs by this evening.

They called a gunda named Irshad to scare me. Before he could threaten me, I threatened him.

You will be the first to go to jail for this, I said. Do not come between us women. This is no fight for a man to interfere in.

He backed out at once.

I had my way because the bednis, for whatever they were worth, were always a little scared of the police. I could tell because I had been through it, and I knew how to have my way with them. I had broken from their cage. They knew what I was capable of.

Do not forget who I am, I reminded them. I was the one who rebelled and walked away free from you bednis.

They brought Laccha from another room. She looked scared. She did not utter a word. She did not cry. She held my hand and we walked out into the sun like warriors.

Did they do anything to you? I asked her.

She just shook her head and said no.

I breathed a huge sigh of relief and hugged her. In that moment, I could see myself in her. I could see my own innocence reflected in her. I could recognize the loss of my own innocence in her. I could recognize in myself a steely exterior that could brace any calamity, but not the tragedy of my story that was about to be repeated. I did not cry. I could not. I had matured so much in that instance alone. I was no longer just her elder sister now. I was her guardian, her mother, her protector. I had to make sure that she went back home as soon as possible with a stern warning to our father to never try these dirty tricks again on us.

She stayed in the kotha with me for a month. Shanna and Dasrath were also living with me at the time. When my chacha came to visit, I told him to take her back.

I do not want to leave, she said. I want to stay with you.

She was the quietest, most shy and soft-spoken girl in our family. She was also beginning to complain of poor eyesight.

Do not worry, I am sending you with chacha; he will ask our mother to take you to a doctor. I have also arranged the money, I told her.

What will you do here? I said. I will see you in Poona when I come visiting.

She did not say anything. Chacha said he would go to his house in Ahmedabad first, and then from there he would take her to Poona. I trusted him. I agreed.

After I few days, I sent a telegram to my mother saying Laccha was going to be back soon.

On their way to Poona from Ahmedabad, when the train halted in Karjat, Laccha got down to drink water from a tap. She failed to board the train back in time. Chacha was sleeping in the compartment when the incident occurred.

Much later, when he woke up in Poona, he rushed to tell my mother what had happened. Laccha was missing. But he did not know at which station she'd got down. The train he had taken had only a few stops on its route – starting with the closest, all the way to Ahmedabad. They went looking for her without informing the police, fearing that the chacha would be arrested for his carelessness with a minor. He was sorry for not being more alert. Everyone in the family forgave him for his helplessness, for he was quite old by then. My mother and sisters did not know what else to do. They did not inform me. They were perhaps scared that I would abandon them out of anger. I was funding the weddings of my sisters, so that none of them should be sold. A few months later, when I went to Poona, they told me what happened in person. It was one of the darkest moments of my life. I could have held myself responsible, but doing anything reckless would endanger my other helpless sisters and the two siblings living with me in the kotha.

I took the same train to Ahmedabad to meet my chacha, and when it halted at Karjat, I even stepped out on to the platform, looking as lost as Laccha. I felt as if my own childhood, my own story, had vanished, but here I was, standing for it, giving it shape with my own instinct to survive. To survive what, I did not know.

What I did know was that I was living for my sisters and brother. I could not protect Laccha, but her loss also meant that I had to look after myself even more now. I had to be smart, careful, brave. Her disappearance was my shadow abandoning me. I could not let such a thing happen again. At the sound of the whistle, I boarded the train, my shadow following me. I think the loss was too great and too invisible at the same time. I could stop and grieve or I could move on like nothing had happened. It reaffirmed my faith in myself. I was too strong to let go. I looked out of the window. No one was waving goodbye. But a part of me was always going to wander on this platform, lost and looking to board a train back to life. Laccha, the simple and beautiful girl with poor eyesight, disappeared into the mist of our memories with time. She could not find her way out of the dense fog of her cursed destiny. My mother did not give up looking for her, inquiring at all the stations on the route. Many years later, she found out that Laccha had met a tea vendor on the platform, who had married her. They had two children. The husband did not allow Laccha out of the house, fearing she would get lost again. He did not trust her eyesight. No one got to see her. My mother decided not to pursue the matter, but never stopped checking on Laccha's status. She died a few years after settling down with the vendor. It was rumoured that he had killed her. We also heard that she died of grief. We did not find out what happened exactly. Her life remained a mystery to all of us, perhaps to herself as well – a clear case of lost and never found.

In Bandook Gully, where my fame was growing, Qamar aapa, a bai in Muzaffarpur, called me to perform at a wedding function, or as we called it, lagan ka beeda, for selective and trusted private parties. She would sing. I would dance. We worked as a team. She had seen me dance in Calcutta. She wanted to partner with me because she was ageing. She needed to infuse her mujra with some young blood.

We toured throughout Bihar – Katihar, Chhapra, Motihari Zila, Bakhtiyarpur, Begusarai and Patna. We had to be careful because, most times, these parties were held in isolated locations. We did not like to travel far from city limits as Bihar was notorious for goons. Once, when I was at Qamar aapa's house in Muzaffarpur, she got a request from a party for a performance in Bakhtiyarpur. The party said they would pay a fat sum of fifteen thousand rupees. She asked me to dance. I said all right. Take the beeda. Take the contract. Cash in advance. A jeep arrived to take us to the venue. The performance was to be held in an MLA's farmhouse. I did not know his name. I did not care. Hoga koi, neta-pheta! Must be some politician! We did not care for politics. The party was quite decent. We had to perform for two nights. The first night went fine, without any disruption. We danced to Bhojpuri songs. Some were risqué numbers: '*Hum na jaibe sasur ghar*', '*Phulori bina chatni*', '*Jeth ki doopehri*'. On the second night, some dacoits carrying rifles, faces covered with a saafa, entered the premises. I was dancing at the time.

A man approached me. Aye, he said. Kya karat hai? What are you doing?

I could not understand his boli, language, but could sense that he was interrogating me in his querulous voice.

Two dacoits came up on stage and said, You will have to dance for us now.

Do something for us, the sardar said.

Tu humka jaanat nahi ho nachaniya, he said. Hum kaun hai? You, dancer, you don't know who I am.

My fearlessness had begun to spring up in dire situations.

Haan, kya baat hai? Kaun hai aap? I boldly asked. What is the matter? Who are you?

I thought he would fire a bullet into the sky to announce his name. He did not.

Please me, he said. Then I will tell you who I am.

I consulted the ustads. They asked if I knew any song for dacoits.

I used to reside in Bandook Gully. How could I not know any such songs?

I danced to *'Baat karte hain jab mashooq se, kaam lete nahi bandook se'*.

He was mighty pleased. After the performance, he said, Can you see that white jeep standing there?

He pointed at a vehicle parked some distance away.

Yes, I said.

Quietly go and sit in it, he said.

Why? I asked.

Just do as I say or you will repent, he said.

It was happening just like in the movies.

I walked towards the jeep, but as I was approaching it, I turned left and ran towards a room. He was a few paces behind me and he caught up, and before I could bolt the door, he barged in and shut it from inside.

I was trapped.

She is mine – she will go with me, he shouted.

Qamar aapa, who was outside, began howling. She begged the MLA to rescue me.

Luckily, the MLA's boys outnumbered the four or five dacoits outside. They quickly overpowered the bandits.

The dacoit who was inside the room with me did not want to harm me. He wanted to be with me. He did not try to rape me, because his men were taking a beating outside. His plan was to find a way to get out of the room. He understood that he was the one trapped, not me. The MLA stood outside the door and threatened him. If you touch the girl, you will go to jail. If you let her go, I will let you go. I will call the police if you do not open the door.

The sardar opened the door.

I will see how you leave this town, he said.

I rushed out to Qamar aapa. She saw that my bluster had only been a clumsy tact to confuse the opponent. I did not know my own move after that. I was visibly shaken. My face was sorry for trying to outsmart the powerful. We wept. The young men felt sorry for us. We were vulnerable. Just us two women. They sent us back in their jeep. They did not take the obvious route from Bakhtiyarpur to Muzaffarpur.

The dacoits might follow you, they said.

The men took another route and took us to Patna railway station.

When I boarded the train, I asked Qamar aapa, Who was that daaku?

Kya pata? Who knows? she said. Everyone has a gun here.

Bihar was a rough terrain for us. It was full of bandits. Another time, when we reached a venue for a performance, we realized there was no venue. The party had called us to a deserted location where there were no lights. They turned on the headlights of their jeeps and I had to dance in that filmy set-up. Men sat on the ground and watched, drinking and shooting into the sky. If I remember right, they wanted some vulgar song and the lyrics went something like this: 'Lutan lutan lagi barah baras ki ladki lutan lagi.' I did not enjoy performing there, but I did give it my best, because I knew I would be harassed for a clumsy show if I allowed my fear to get the better of me. In these situations, one had to put up a brave front – sometimes even behave raucously like the audience – to make them feel that we were not going to be intimidated by their bullets.

We used to be heckled a lot in Bihar. It was a rough and tough terrain. Our kajal, lipstick, powder melted in the heat and sometimes in fright. Men flaunted guns everywhere we went. Random firings frightened me, but I continued dancing with a deaf ear to the ringing bullets. Qamar aapa sat in one corner, singing. I was the one doing all the tamasha. Once, a man became obsessive in Begusarai. After a performance, he stalked me.

Your performance wrapped up early, he said. I paid you for the whole day. Now, spend the rest of the time with me in another location.

This was not the deal, I told the pimp.

The stalker wanted me to sit with him in his car.

She will – she is the shy kind, the pimp said. But not in the car, please; she prefers a more private space.

The pimp told the stalker to lead the way in his vehicle.

Do not panic, the pimp told me.

Qamar aapa and I were trying not to show it on our worried faces. I do not know how, but the pimp sped up and took a detour by driving into a jungle, making the stalker and his men lose sight of our vehicle. As we got away, a nervous smile began to appear on our faces: the ustads, Qamar aapa and I. Just when we were prepared to breathe a sigh of relief, like in the movies, the jeep broke down in the middle of the jungle. We had run out of petrol. The sun had gone down. We did not have a torch. How were we going to get out of here alive? It was winter. Darr ke maare humari halat kharab! Fear made us sweat. We crept out of the jeep, in search of a light. We walked for what seemed liked an eternity till we reached a hut.

The pimp spoke the local dialect.

Darwaza khola ho, he said. Mehmaan aayat rahe. Paani peeye lagi. Open the door; we are visitors and we are thirsty for water.

A voice spoke from inside the hut.

There is a well outside. There is a lota, tumbler, and a glass. Use it.

The door did not open. It must have been around two in the morning.

We did not want to make any movement in the grass. What if someone else was following us? The man inside the hut heard absolute silence in response. So he decided to open the door and let us in. The pimp told us not to worry. He said he would go to the highway as soon as dawn broke. It was one of the most harrowing nights of our lives. The old man snuffed out the lamp in his hut. We prayed all night. In the morning, the pimp found a truck driver who helped him get petrol. We went to a dhaba after that, freshened up and ate breakfast in the open, sunning our clammy hearts.

In Muzaffarpur, I faced stiff competition from the local bais. Once, I had to compete with Neelu, Rani and Shamsa Bano. A party had organized an event where all of them were called and asked to perform one after the other. Shamsa went up first. Rani was number two. She was a superb singer and dancer. '*Chahe toh mora jiya le,*' she sang and roused the crowd. Both the bais received a fantastic reception. A fight erupted in the audience. The men were raucous. Guns blazed. Peeye-khaay log karte hain uddhambaazi. Drunk men create a scene. The ustads began to panic. These girls were too good. They understood the mood of the crowd. They knew how to work it. How would Rekha, an outsider, match them, they wondered. Allah jis ko rakkhe, usko kaun chakhe? Who can touch those whom Allah protects? I told the announcer to let me go third. I wanted to be done and slip out before the last performance. It was getting colder as the night descended on our shoulders, coating our bodies with dew. Ustad Aamir, who was on the harmonium, said, What will happen now? Ghomey bhi nahi milenge. We won't even get any money. Ghomey was our code word for money. Loorey toh bokhla gaye, said the ustad. The patrons have gone berserk. The announcer used the opportunity to introduce me. She is a new girl – please welcome her in your hearts, he said. The crowd wanted to see me now. They knew the others, who were regular performers. I sang and danced. '*Sanam tu bewafa ke naam se mashoor ho jaaye.*' Notes were showered on us. We made about five thousand rupees that night. Aamir bhai did not expect so much love and cash. As soon as we collected the money onstage, I asked the announcer to quickly call on their local favourite, Neelu, so that we could wrap up backstage and scoot. I wrapped a shawl around me, sat in a jeep with my ustads and left. If we had waited for the programme to end, the crowd would not have let us leave in peace. Still, some of the men chased us for a short distance, shouting at us to come back. Soon, they faded into the night, as did we.

Shifting to Bandook Gully had opened up many doors for me, but there was nuisance there too. When Phullo came to Bandook Gully, she started creating trouble for everyone. She had a room built on one side. She was quite competitive. She was beautiful, and good at singing and dancing, but she was a gundi, criminal, by nature. Mijaaz ki gundi thi. I think she was called Phullo because she was plump and walked around in a huff. Har dam phooli hui thi. She was always puffy. With Phullo around, I tried to spend most of my time downstairs. There was another Meena who lived on the ground floor. This Meena was not classically good-looking and, in those days, she was called kaali, saanwli, dark. She did not sing or dance well, maybe because of her own lack of confidence. Because I was friendly with the older tawaifs in Meena's house, we also got along well. I think she looked up to me, so that made it easier for her to become my chaperone or for me to become hers, in a manner of speaking. I took her to the cinema, to restaurants, to New Market for shopping. She also became my confidante. Girls who had taken plots on the terrace got their rooms constructed there. In a year or so, the terrace was buzzing with activity from five rooms. The older, senior singers downstairs were on their way out. Times were changing. People wanted masti, fun. Garam khoon. Hot blood. Disco ka zamaana aa gaya tha. It was the era of disco music. Baby and Meera replaced the two sisters, Lakshmi and Geeta, upstairs. This Geeta is not the same as the other Geeta living downstairs. There was a constant flux of tawaifs coming and going as it suited them. Many tawaifs and even ustads have the same name, so it is confusing to address them correctly. Often we referred to them by the kotha's number prefixed to their name like ekyasi-wali Meena.

Kishori, an old eunuch, used to visit us in Bandook Gully. He used to tell us stories about other kothas, carrying gossip and singing folk songs. He used to wear soorma, bindiya and chuttiya, a tassel in his braided hair. Arre o, mere ko diyo paise. Give me some money, he used to say when the patrons came in the evening. He tried to sing in mujras, so some of us would let him entertain the men between our breaks. A ten-rupee note was enough to shut him up. We gave him food and our old sarees. When he got too old, he returned to his hometown, Mahabaleshwar. Phullo did not like him. She kept making trouble – fighting with him, with us and with many patrons. She would sometimes thrash her own lovers. She had three children, a girl and two boys, all from different men. She was 'kept' by those men at different stages in her life. She had sent her children to boarding schools in Kalimpong and Kurseong. She would sometimes try to lure other rich patrons into her room for a game of cards and liquor. That was how it would start. She did not like to sing and dance. It probably bored her or was too much effort for her when she knew that ultimately all the men wanted was intimacy. So she changed tack. The other girls were not like her. If someone was a keep, she belonged to that man alone. He would arrive every night to be entertained, either with his friends or all by himself. Phullo would not entertain new patrons. But most girls also knew that such an arrangement would not last forever.

In those days, a man who sold gemstones used to come to chat with me at noon. Since we did not really have much time to go out a lot, except on some holidays and dry days, men used to visit us during the day, selling gems, sarees, toiletries, all kinds of knick-knacks for the house. Apart from the gajra seller, the chanawala, the phuchkawala, the paanwala, the biscuit-cakewala, the sabziwala, the gaddiwala, the kitaabwala, the dhobi, the bhisti, the mehtar, we had an entire supermarket thronging the building all day.

This gemstone seller, whose name I have forgotten, was a friend to a lot of patrons too. One night, Husn Bano, a famous singer who lived below my room, invited everyone from the kotha to her house to celebrate her birthday. We were not on the best of terms. She was a snob. She had previously made faces at my presence in a few hotel gigs, where we used to land up to perform in rooms for big parties.

We had once performed for film director Shakti Samanta in a hotel room. She was aware of my dance, but was not too fond of my singing. She was rude and gossiped about me. And yet, when the invite was sent, it was for everyone. I did not go. I pretended to be sick when the other girls asked me to join them. I shut my door, pulled a blanket over my head and heard the din from downstairs. I knew that the local goons were also invited to the party, which was the bigger reason why I did not want to socialize. Mohammad Omar, Rab, their boys – it was a whole gang of rogues. Some women enjoyed mixing with danger. I did not. It so happened that the gemstone jeweller was also at the party. His friends, Rehmat, Kayoom and Siraj, were with him. These men lived in Machua Bazaar. I think they were overwhelmed with the boisterous crowd at the party, so they decided to come upstairs. The jeweller knocked on my door.

Arre aap, I opened half a door and said, Aaj toh bandh hai. Business is shut today.

Paani toh pilao, the jeweller said, opening the other half panel of the door to invite himself in. The other men followed him in. I was not dressed in finery, my hair out of place, my saree was ordinary cotton. Even the gaddi was not in place.

The men seemed drunk. They made themselves comfortable. I sent a servant, Madan, to fetch cold drinks for everyone.

Suddenly, Rehmat said, Sunaiye na kuch. Please sing for us.

He was a tall man with a defined jaw. He had a thick moustache, curly hair and was simply dressed in a bush shirt and trousers. His crisp voice was clear even in the lowest register.

I had expected one of them to request a song. So I said, Nahi, aaj nahi; neeche awaaz jayegi toh bura maan legi. Not tonight; people partying downstairs will be offended.

I knew if Husn Bano heard sounds from my window she would be upset.

Theek hai, he said. Kal aayein toh? Okay. If we come tomorrow?

Haan, I said. Yes.

The next day, he arrived with his friends. Rehmat enjoyed my mujra. He would hum along in a few songs. And then he sang 'Kabhi toh miloge jeevan saathi', as if he was looking for one, while, at the time, he was a married man. He followed it with 'Mere mehboob'. I was flustered at first, then tried to laugh when he sang 'Radhike tune bansuri churayi', directed at me. The interruptions happened so frequently that by the time he sang 'Ajhun na aaye baalma' I wanted him to take my place in the mujra and sing to the audience, or maybe it was a performance he was putting up for me, wooing me in my own kotha in the middle of my performance. I must say I was half-charmed, but half-irritated as well. I would only find out later that this was his style with every tawaif. I was not special. He wanted the attention far more than some of us who did it for lack of an alternative. He used to be a regular patron of Mallika in her prime at building number five. He was from an affluent background. He had five brothers. He was probably the youngest, and the most gregarious. In those days, he was in love with a Maharashtrian girl named Rupa, who had either spurned his advances or left the city. I am not too sure what transpired. He began drinking a lot to overcome his grief. He was the archetype patron jo gham bhulane ke liye peeta aur gaata hai – one who drinks and sings to drown his woes. He started coming to me regularly. He gave me gifts, a tanpura, sarees and a shawl on Eid. He grew fond of me maybe because I am also from Maharashtra. It took less time for him to propose marriage than it probably took to forget Rupa.

Humse nikaah kar lo, he said. Marry me.

What? I said.

Humse nikah kar lo.

If you say it one more time, it will become serious like you mean it, I said.

Humse nikah kar lo.

He repeated it thrice – the number of times for me to say 'qubool hai' for such a marriage to be sanctified. But it would always remain unlawful outside the kotha. If he really meant it, I would have to convert. I was not ready to do that. I said no. I said we could be a couple in the kotha. I could not see myself turning into a ba-purdah, veiled housewife.

I want to see your wife first, I said.

Why? he asked.

Aise hi, just like that, I said. Then I will tell you if we can marry.

How can I trust you? he asked.

You cannot, I said. You will have to take a risk.

When I said that, he understood that my intention was not to disrupt his marriage. I just wanted to see his wife to know if I was worth the trouble as his second trophy.

Okay, he said, I will bring Husna.

Husna, I contemplated. Beauty was engraved in her name.

We arrived like strangers in a movie hall showing *Khoon Pasina*. We spotted each other in the lobby. I saw that Husna was a short, small, fair and beautiful woman – wrapped in a saree like a doll in a box. And here I was, walking tall, proud and more social than her. She looked very much the dutiful ba-purdah housewife. I definitely did not see myself becoming her.

I had told Rehmat to meet me at the snacks counter during intermission. He came alone. We were chatting and laughing. I told him she was fit for him. Just then, Husna, out of nowhere, came out.

Where is the toilet? she asked him.

He showed her the way. She had seen us talking, so we had to wait till her return to allay her suspicion.

When she returned, Rehmat introduced her as Husna.

Aur yeh, and she … He looked at me.

Rekha, I said.

The film's poster, featuring the heroine Rekha was looming in the background. I was wearing jhumkas, a gajra, a floral-print saree in green and red, with a big red tika on my forehead and plum-red lipstick. Husna was beautiful but plain. I had what Husna seemed to lack at the moment – a persona, and looks that were more glamourous and attractive than her. But I also felt sad about her masoomiyat, her innocence. What would become of her if I took Rehmat away? In a way, I felt a sisterly kinship with her – her being robbed of a life of dignity and grace. I did not want to be a homebreaker.

Can I get that change for the hundred rupees I gave you? I asked Rehmat.

He understood what I meant. He pulled out two fifty-rupee notes from his wallet. I took them, said bye and walked across for popcorn and a cold drink.

He returned to his seat. Husna asked him about me.

She was just a stranger looking for change, he said to her.

Where is her hundred-rupee note? she asked him.

He had to show her a note. I had not given him any money.

He pulled a note out of his wallet. She took it and tore it.

Aisi aurton ka paisa haraam hai, she said. Money belonging to
such women is a sin.

I laughed heartily when Rehmat told me later what happened.
Husna wasn't as innocent as I had thought. She would be fine.

Poor Rehmat, ghaate ka sauda ho gaya! What a loss he bargained!

Rehmat did not insist on marriage for a while. We went to Sagar
and Ambar for dinner. We went to Lighthouse, Paradise and Orient
for movies. He did not spend a lot of money. Sometimes, I used
to pay for us. Meena and her patron, Sitaram, would tag along.
He would pay for all four of us. I think it was around this same
time that I met the world-famous sarangi player Ustad Sultan Khan.
He was not world-famous yet. His chacha, whose name I cannot
recollect at the moment – was it Basheer? – used to play the sarangi
in my mujra. One time, the great Sultan Khan came from Bombay
to meet him. His chacha brought him to Bandook Gully. I did not
know he was a famous man. I thought he was like the other ustads,
who played the sarangi in Bombay's kothas.

He was a jovial man to talk to. The ustads gathered around
him. Some ustads had played on the radio. It was then that I
heard that Lata Mangeshkar had asked Sultan Khan to play the
sarangi in one of her performances. A mehfil was organized in
Sunita's room in Bandook Gully, where the ustads and the bais
gave nazrana, a monetary gift, for his performance. He played
some classical Indian raags I was not familiar with, but since all
the ustads were so clued in and saying 'wah wah', the bais, too, did
the same. A few days later, when I was performing with his chacha
for a party, he sneaked in behind me, took the sarangi from his
chacha and played. I was singing a ghazal by Ghalib that Amir
bhai had taught me – 'Har ek baat pe kehte ho tum ki tu kya hai'.
I noticed much later, when I turned around to put some notes
given by a patron into a gullak behind me, that Khan saab was
playing the sarangi. In his smile, I could sense more than just love

for his art. I could feel his eyes on the back of my neck. He would come to meet me often. He never said it, but we know how to read a man's body language. I was clear about one thing – ustads sit behind us, what can they give us? They can only take from us. I was not like the other bais who fell in love with the ustads. Yes, some of them were handsome; they came in the evenings, dressed in the crispest kurtas and even wore kaajal in their eyes. I also knew that once a bai fell for an ustad, he would control her. All her hard work would be worthless. What we have with the ustads is a choli-daman ka saath, an unspoken understanding, but it's better not to soil it. Ishara and nazar, hints and glances, are important to convey our message to them in a mehfil, a social gathering, when we need to instruct them about tempo in a tune – and that is how we should maintain our relationship. Ustad Sultan Khan met me a few more times when he visited the city. He understood that I was not going to fall for his fame or his charming words.

A tabla player in Calcutta, Mohammed Ali, also tried his luck with me. He was persistent. Bade hasraton se dekhta tha woh mujhe. With such yearning he used to look at me. He was tall, fair, had broad shoulders, a thick and firm moustache, and a fairly impressionable personality with a deep, baritone voice.

One day, he said, There is a good film playing in New Cinema; let us go.

Okay, I said.

I was being a sport about it. He thought he would take me to a film, spend some money on me and I would fall for him. Hah! I was smarter than that. We went to see the film *Bindiya Aur Bandook*, starring Joginder. It was about dacoits and damsels. It was awful, but entertaining because the audience was tickled. When I was preparing to travel to Delhi for my annual visit to the Nizamuddin Auliya shrine during the month of Urs, he decided to tag along with me, saying he could show me his family home in Saharanpur.

We went to meet his family. We then went to the dargah of Qutub Sahib in Delhi. There, he said to me, Please forgive me. You have a jolly nature. I was misreading it for something else. You are my sister from today. I laughed and said, What do you mean? Was I supposed to make something else of our friendship? He felt sorry for himself. You are not like the other girls, he said. Ustads always went for the single girls first. I was used to living independently. I did not have a guardian. I was easy prey to many, but I also thought of my single status as an advantage to be able to make my own decisions. That is how I knew how to be observant, to not be influenced by the opinions of others and to study the nature of men.

On the one hand, there were ustads trying to woo me, and on the other, I had a villain in the background trying to ruin my life. Phullo was jealous of my name and fame. She had started insinuating that I was a baanjh, a barren woman, that my womb would always be dry. She had three children. I obviously could not match it. I had been with Rehmat, but I was not able to conceive. It had begun to worry me a lot.

Mujhe baccha chahiye, I want a baby, Rehmat! I said to him.

He smiled and perhaps thought that having a baby would make me marry him as well. He was more than happy that a woman in the kotha found him desirable and wanted to have his baby. At the same time, my dhanda was doing so well that I could have quit at my peak and settled down as a keep. Phullo was right. I did not have a child, and seeing most girls there with kids, I felt left out. After the patrons left, after the musicians left, whom did I have to call my own family? I looked after my younger sister, my youngest brother, but they would make their own homes in Poona some day. I was less a sibling and more a motherly figure to them. I had grown up so fast that in a few years of my separation from my own family, I was able to become a woman of the world. I even felt independent enough to start my own family – like some of the women in the kotha who came from similar situations. I felt what I was missing now was the mercy of god. I felt the need to be thankful and contribute to society. So I began to visit temples and shrines to feed and clothe the poor. In return, such places gave me immense peace of mind, strength and courage to be moved by faith and serve the less fortunate. Surely the gods would answer my prayers too. Rehmat and I were steady for three years, I think. Despite my attempts, when I was not able to conceive, I decided to check with a doctor if I really was a baanjh. The pipe holding your uterus is weak, he said. We will do a small operation. I was young. I wanted a child desperately. To prove everyone wrong, I did the operation. It was successful.

You go to Ajmer dargah every year, mannat maang – ask for a baby, Mallika aapa said.

I thought about what she said. I dreamt of a lemon sitting on a pile of jamun. I picked it up. In another dream, I saw a silver maqbara, where angels were flying. I saw a saint descend and greet me. He gave me an ashy powder. I ate it. He told me to drink water from a well. I did. He said to go home and not turn back. When I turned around, I thought I heard the sound of khadak, wooden slippers, following me. I had plucked white jasmine flowers from a bough and was walking back home. The dream felt as if Khwaja Garib Nawaz was calling me to Ajmer. I attended the Urs festival at the dargah of Khwaja Moinuddin Chishti in Ajmer and asked for a mannat. I asked for a child. I was pregnant in the month of Ramzan. I was dancing when I felt light-headed from a twirl. I took a break, asking another tawaif to take over. I puked and smiled to myself. I returned to my performance and completed it happily. I knew my prayer had been answered. It felt like a gift from God. I was so happy that initially all I did was spend time outside. I did not feel like working. I wanted to be free and celebrate. I saw a lot of films in theatres. Amitabh Bachchan's films in which Rekha was with him: *Muqaddar Ka Sikander, Khoon Pasina, Do Anjaane, Alaap,*

Mr Natwarlal, Ganga Ki Saugand and *Suhaag*. In those days, theatres played both old and new releases interchangeably. I saw some films more than once. Maybe I was imagining myself as Rekha. You were also kicking inside me and dancing. Maybe even you wanted to come out and watch the movies with me. Since I was a thin girl, I could not carry the weight of this beautiful gift as smoothly as some of the other curvy girls. The sixteenth and seventeenth day of the month used to be painful. A nurse told me that the baby was in danger of slipping out.

I decided to get admitted to Lohia Matri Seva Sadan Hospital. From the third month, I stayed there. Shekhar had taken me to the hospital and got me admitted. Now here is the bit I forgot to mention earlier. When I moved to Bandook Gully from ekyasi number after my fight with Inder bhaiya and Munni, I had briefly lost touch with Shekhar. When he eventually found out about my relocation, which was just a matter of time for him, he came to see me in Bandook Gully. Around this time, Rehmat had entered the picture. Slowly, Rehmat and I became close, and Shekhar, being a very wise man, saw it and took two steps back, allowing me to decide whom I wanted to spend time with. Shekhar was always around when I had a fight with Rehmat. It so happened that when I was having complications during my pregnancy, Shekhar was around to give me the care and attention I needed then. Rehmat's erratic behaviour was also the main reason Shekhar was always there to support me. I had a room to myself in the hospital. After a few days, Rehmat came to visit me. Then, his friends started visiting. One day, his friend Eshwar said to me, Bhabhi, Khan saab toh Bimla ke paas jaate hain. Sister-in-law, Khan saab has gone to Bimla's kotha. Let him go, I said. I was not going to stop him. How could I? I was not going to marry him. I did not want to live in purdah. I preferred my present lifestyle. Of course, the news affected me, but who was I to dictate terms to Rehmat?

My servant, Madan, used to come to visit me with home-cooked meals. He was the only family I had in those days. Shanna and Dasrath were back in Poona. In the seventh month, my condition began deteriorating. One evening, there was a cyclone in the city and I felt one inside me. The doctors advised to shift me to the labour room. That day, when Rehmat came, we had an argument about his visits to the kotha.

I was in pain, and I was dealing with a man who I knew was not the loyal, faithful kind. You can have the baby, but do not give the baby my name, he said in a fit of anger and left. I was in such pain that Doctor Khatri said to prepare the operation room for a Caesarean section. When I was being wheeled into the operating room that evening, my condition was so critical that a doctor was saying that they could save only one of us. Save me, I said. I do not want the child. Save me. Who would look after the child if I died? Without a mother, and a father who didn't want to be present, what would become of that baby? I could have another if I lived.

Save my life, doctor, I said.

Doctor Bohra arrived – she was a lovely woman who always spoke to me in the gentlest voice. What happened, Rekha? she asked when she walked into the operation room. She caressed my head and tried to reassure me.

You be patient, she said, smiling. You will be fine.

Seeing her look so relaxed made me feel even more anxious. I started blabbering, knowing perhaps that she was there to support me.

Didi, I said, save me.

Do not worry, she said, You are fine. If you do not have a normal delivery, I will operate on you. I have made all the necessary arrangements.

She placed a machine on my back and did something to turn your head down as you had moved up by then. She kept talking to me while the old nurses around her massaged my body, helping me breathe and push. You were delivered at dawn, like a beam of light shooting out of me after a very dark night. It was the most painful experience of my life, but it also gave me the most relief. I looked at you as Bohra dangled you in front of me and said, See, Rekha, you have a boy.

I passed out, saying, Didi, save me.

Rehmat was informed about your birth in the evening. He came to see me. I had a daiyya named Pushpa in my room. She looked after me.

You were missing from my room. I had prayed for a girl, but Khwaja baba had given me a boy. It was unexpected, but I didn't care too much about the sex of the baby. What mattered most was that I was fertile. That was more important to me. I could have more children if I wanted in the future. I could prove to the bais that I was no baanjh.

After two days of rest, I asked her, Pushpa, where is my child?

The baby is too weak, they have put him in an incubator, she said.

You were a premature baby, small and weak, born before your time, so you had to be kept in intensive medical care.

I had telegrammed my mother in Poona. She arrived after five days with Shanna and Dasrath. The girls from the kotha came to see me. A week passed by like this. There was no sign of you, though. The nurses kept telling me that you were not well.

One day, as I was resting in my room, Babaji visited me. Ajmer-wale baba came in my dream that day. Then I saw my Kali Mata telling me to leave. I noticed the gods were on one side and Yamraj stood on another side.

Take the child with you and leave from here, the gods said. They looked worried and angry. They pointed to Yamraj, saying he would take the child away if I did not.

The next morning, I got up and said, I want to leave.

You cannot leave now – you are not well and neither is your child, a nurse said. She would not let me see my baby.

When Rehmat arrived, I said, Take me home now. Right now.

Doctor Bohra had asked me to wait for a few more days. But I was not willing to listen.

The baby will die if he is not given special treatment, she told me.

I will sign the leaving forms at my risk, I said. I want my baby now, and I am leaving this very moment.

They brought you to me when they realized that I was not going to listen to anyone. I signed the papers saying that the baby was being taken away at the patient's risk.

I held you in my hands. You were so small and light, like a toy. I had given birth to something so thin and frail. I wept and kissed and hugged you, like I had touched the ultimate gift of God. I had not only survived childbirth, but I understood that I was capable of nourishing life inside me when I was living my own life like a dead person. Now I had the biggest reason to live, to be happy for myself, for you, for the two of us alone. I promised you then that I would not let anything come between us.

When we sat in the car, the journey from Lohia Matri Seva Sadan Hospital to Bandook Gully felt like forever. The taxi was stuck in a jam for hours. I wanted to walk. I could wait no longer to get home. I had been lying in a hospital bed for four months.

The nightmare I had a day before began manifesting in real life. Everywhere I looked, it felt like someone or something was attacking us, trying to obstruct us from reaching a safe place.

My mother was astonished to see me home. She was not expecting me for a few weeks. She had been told that the mother would make it home, but there was no certainty for the child.

She was happy to see us both. She heated water for a bath. I was finally able to take a breath at home and finally felt at peace. I felt the vibe change in my favour. You were in my arms and I was holding you with such pride, with such joy – this was an achievement that the girls in the kotha thought I was not capable of.

I whispered in your ear, My only love, my child, my everything. I will die to see you live. I will do everything in my might to see that you get the best love and care in the world. You special child, you saved me. I remembered the lorie '*Tu mere saath rahega munne*' that I had watched in the film *Trishul* when you were in my belly. I gently cradled you in my arms.

The tag of a baanjh was removed from my name in the market. I was not up for distress sale any more. I had proven my worth.

Khair, anyway, tu toh khwaja baba ki daen hai. You are a gift from the Khwaja Garib Nawaz of Ajmer. I accepted you as you were. In the kotha, a girl is more precious than a boy. She is the one who takes over business when we retire and looks after us. What will a boy do? I had seen the sons of kothewalis. They were useless. Wastrels! All they did was loaf around, indulge in pimping, alcohol, drugs, randibaazi and gundagardi, womanizing and hooliganism. But not once did I have this thought, What will I do with a boy? I had seen how my mother had raised Dasrath. Maybe that is what I needed to do. My mother was very happy to get another male child to fuss over. She oiled your bones, fed you, bathed you and played with you like you were her little one.

A girl child's birth is celebrated in the kotha with great pomp. I wanted to do the same for you. I wanted to do it as a way to thank the gods too, and to serve the people, including preparing a feast that would be distributed among the poor. The pandit who made your janam kundli, birth chart, said that I should name you Mohan. I found it a little old-fashioned. I named you Manish instead. I do not recollect who suggested the name. Maybe it was the masterji who used to teach me Hindi.

After about two months of your birth, when I wanted to do a jalsa for your delayed chhati ceremony, the sixth-day celebration after your birth, I needed some money. I asked Rehmat for it.

I needed some twenty-five or thirty thousand to organize a feast for the women and my friends in the kotha. It was going to be a grand affair. Rehmat said he did not have so much money and that he needed to go to his village in Chhapra for some urgent work.

I prayed to the Ajmer-wale baba.

Meri laaj rakh lena, guard my honour, I said.

I made do with less money.

For your jalsa, I had a deg, pot, of biryani cooked by party food caterers. A deg of zarda, sweet rice, was cooked. Ghol, buttermilk, was prepared. Chairs were put out in the street, in the kotha, on the terrace. The building was lit with lights and festoons. It was an event that was both grand and dignified – there was no loud music or dancing, just an orderly and quiet feast to mark a baby's arrival.

But since I was the mother who could not stop grinning, how could the event go on without my performance? Everyone wanted to see the mother dance. It was decided that I would do a quick mujra in each of the rooms in the kotha. No other girl would perform that day. It was a way for the patrons to gift money for the child's well-being. Shekhar arrived for the event. Rehmat also arrived uninvited.

Shekhar mere liye bahut saara badhawa laaye thay. Shekhar had brought a lot of gifts for me. His hamper had silk sarees, dry fruits, seasonal fruits and gold ornaments. Rehmat came empty-handed and felt guilty seeing how loved I was by the other patrons. I was irritated by his presence. Rehmat started drinking and behaving callously with others and followed me from one room to another. Every once in a while, when I took a break between the rooms, I would check on the guests as well, watching from the balcony and feeling a swell of pride that all was going well with the dinner. Everyone in the mohalla was welcome. Some goons of Omar had also turned up. Some people from the neighbourhood were upset about the presence of goons. A loud argument followed in the street. When I heard of it, I stopped mid-performance to address the situation. Geeta was trailing me everywhere I went. She stopped me from stepping out, fearing it would only escalate the situation. She was right.

On one side, there was Rehmat, annoying me with his behaviour, and on the other side, some hoodlums were about to ruin my party. But if I did not take stock of the situation now, it would leave a bad impression on my standing as the hostess of the event. It was an opportunity for me to set things right. If I could handle it, Rehmat could be dismissed with ease too. Since I was wearing a lot of jewellery, Geeta took off my ornaments before I went out in the street to handle the fight. I wrapped my shoulders in my aanchal and walked downstairs. I managed to speak politely to the belligerent men and calmed down the angry guests.

Aaj kothe mein mere ladke ki khushi ka jalsa hai; aap log se guzarish hai uski salamati ke liye dua karein, I said. Today is my son's sixth-day ceremony; I request you to please pray for his well-being.

Everyone gathered understood that the evening was not about them and moved on. A young man, Fazal, who worked in a nearby hotel used to respect me a lot, so he helped disperse the crowd immediately. I ushered the goons to the terrace, where they were served food without a fuss. It was then that I found out that Phullo had invited the goons to attend the jalsa. She was trying to disrupt it. I was in no mood to start another fight.

Around one in the morning, Rehmat was still sitting in my room. My mother looked at him and said in her pede ki bhasha, Yeh kai ko thonka hai yahan? Why is he still here?

She said to him to futtay – get lost. I told him and his chamcha to leave.

Rehmat told me, I made a mistake – I did not get any gifts.

You have done no wrong – I was not expecting anything from you, I said.

His admission of guilt was my gift. After that I never looked at him the same way I did before. He was a guest in his own son's celebration party. That day onwards, he became Khan saab to me, a patron, and not the father of my child. I began calling him Khan saab to distance myself from him.

The next evening, he returned, occupying my room with his group of friends. They would not leave, no matter what I said. It felt like they were harassing me. My patrons began to move into the other rooms, seeing that my room was already full of men. It was Khan saab's tactic to make me give in to his demands.

Sometimes, with the help of another tawaif, we would distract his men and make them leave. At other times, we quarrelled and pushed them out. Fights erupted. It began to get dirty when he began sneaking into the small room that had a separate entrance and a sliding door connecting it to the main room. My mother would be sitting inside there, attending to you while I performed. He would pinch you, slap you, find ways to make you cry so that my mujra would be interrupted by the sound of your wail and I would have to leave mid-performance. You know, it was just like that song 'Jinhe naaz hai' in Pyaasa.

> Woh ujle darichon mein payal ki chan chan
> Thaki haari saanson pe tabley ki dhan dhan
> Yeh berooh kamron mein khansi ki than than
> Jinhe naaz hai Hind par woh kahaan hai.

Here we are, struggling to survive in stressful living conditions, upar se logon ki jhanjhat! To top it, harassment from patrons. One thing patrons did not like to see in the kotha in the evenings was a child. They had left their own at home to be there. They did not want to see children running around, or hear them crying. They certainly did not want to be reminded of their domestic lives. The girls would stash their children in lofts in their rooms. I was the only one who had a separate room attached, where my mother, Shanna, Dasrath –

who was also living with me for a while – and you would wait for the mujra to get over.

I had heated confrontations with Khan saab as patrons waited patiently for my return. It affected my performance. In the kotha, word spreads very quickly as the walls are thin and not soundproof. Girls would be secretly happy if my business was going down. The patrons would simply move to their rooms.

Khan saab knew this and was creating trouble for me. My younger sister, brother and mother were equally traumatized by his behaviour. One day, I sent them back to Poona.

Khan saab had also changed his method by then. He stopped visiting every day. This was even more terrifying, since I had no one to take care of you while I performed. What if he landed up suddenly? How would I handle it alone?

I had locked the entrance to the small room from the outside. It deterred Khan saab from accessing the room. Over the next three months, his visits reduced, but they were always marked by fear. During my performances, while you were sleeping in a cot in the small room, I would hear your cries and run to check. I would find you sleeping peacefully. I was hallucinating.

During this time, you had a problem with urination. Your stomach had bloated. I took you to a doctor.

We will have to operate on him – it will be a small fix to help him urinate properly, the doctor said.

He recommended khatna. Circumcision. I took you to a hospital to get it done. Khan saab got word of it. He was happy that I was turning to Islam.

He was telling his chamchas, sycophants, Musalmaani karayi, musalmaani karayi. She has made the boy Muslim. He used to call me Rekhu.

Rekhu ne musalmaani karayi, he claimed.

One evening, I decided to not entertain any patrons. I shut my door and tried to entertain you instead. I knew this was what Khan saab wanted. He wanted me to be at his mercy. When he came, I said, See, now you please stop coming here. I do not want to see your face. I did what was best for my child, not for you.

He was not convinced. He continued to trouble me and, this time, it got worse because he thought I was going to convert to Islam, because how else was I going to raise a Muslim boy?

The girls in the kotha used to call Khan saab 'Totaram' – a singing parrot because he used to interrupt their songs with his own phati awaaz, broken voice. The musicians hated to be in the same room as him. I used to get news that he was sitting in another room, romancing another girl. He was trying to make me jealous or spread gossip about me. The girls began laughing at me, saying I could not keep him happy. It bothered me.

Aap nahi maanenge? You won't behave? I asked. All right, I will leave from here. I will go to Bombay.

Do not take the child with you then, he said.

Where will he stay? I asked.

Put him in an orphanage, he said.

Why? I asked. I will raise my child.

I booked my ticket. You were a few months old by then – still weak and frail. When I reached Howrah station in the evening, I saw that Eshwar, Nathu, Pawan and about five or six more men, along with Khan saab, had followed me.

Bhabhi, aap ghar ja rahi ho? Eshwar asked. Sister-in-law, are you going home?

Yes, I said. I did not tell them that I was going to Bombay to do mujras. I said I was going to my mother's house.

Khan saab looked sober. He smiled and greeted me, and said he wanted to look at you. I was holding you in my arms.

Dikha, dikha, dikha, he said. Show, show, show. He snatched you from me when I showed you to him.

He started walking away from me. I could have panicked and screamed. I did not. He was taking away the only thing I owned and valued in my life. I could see my life being taken away, and I was watching lifelessly, trying to appear calm but breaking from inside. I knew that this was the moment that would define me. If I succumbed, my entire life would be spent at a man's mercy. If I did not, I would remain free to make my own destiny.

As he walked away, he said, Yeh nahi doonga; yeh toh mera baccha hai. Isme mera khoon hai; isse nahi jaane doonga. I won't give him to you; he is mine. He has my blood; I won't let him go.

Do ya chahe nahi do, I said. Give or don't give. I am leaving. I have to leave. You keep the child. Or put him in an orphanage. I do not care.

Mera baanjh hone ka kalank tha, woh ab utar gaya hai. Baba ki meherbaani se main theek hoon, I said. The indignity of being a barren woman does not haunt me any more. By the grace of baba, I am fine. I can make more babies.

I boarded the train.

Eshwar tried to convince Khan saab to give the baby back to his mother.

What will you do with this child? he asked. You already have a family of your own. How will you raise this one? Will it suit your conscience to put the child in an orphanage?

When the train started moving, Khan saab realized what he had done, separating a boy from his mother. He rushed towards me and returned you to me.

I hated him. That was final. I would raise my child without his father and make sure he did not need one. I was enough for my baby.

Bombay

I REACHED MY ELDER SISTER BABBO'S HOUSE IN KALYAN. I STAYED THERE for a week and then told my jijaji, brother-in-law, Anoop, to take me to Bombay.

This is Bombay, he said.

He was slurping on tea, chewing on a khari biscuit in the morning.

Not this one, I said. Bombay, where the girls perform mujra.

He put his cup down and looked at me. He was a good man. Tall, fair, with kind eyes and a polite tone. He had heard of my mujras from my sister, but had never watched them. I gathered that he did not know where the mujras of Bombay took place. But he did not show the slightest hint of ignorance.

What will you do there? he asked.

Naach gaana, I said. I will sing and dance.

I told him about Congress House. I told him to find out where it was. He nodded and said he would arrange for a trip.

We were going to embark on the trip of a lifetime. I was nervous and excited.

I had leased out my room in Bandook Gully to Sarita, a girl in the kotha. I told her to pay the rent to the bariwala on time. I would return if I felt like after a few months.

One day, Anoop jija and I boarded a train from Kalyan to VT station. When we arrived there, I was suddenly aware of entering a very big world. The station is so massive with oonchi chhath aur British-zamaane ki banawat – high ceilings and colonial architecture – that I felt like it was a portal through which we were entering a whole new world.

I was excited because this was what I wanted to do. I had a junoon, passion, to do better in life, to succeed in my line of work. And Bombay was where the real money was, where the real adventure was.

From there we took a taxi to the Congress House area near Grant Road. The taxiwala knew exactly where it was. We reached the venue and saw a signboard with 'Bombay Sangeet Kalakar Mandal' written on the gate. It was a narrow entrance leading into a compound. The gate was imposing and deserted in the afternoon, which I immediately understood and relaxed because kothas are usually quiet at this hour.

I had heard that the tawaifs of the kothas in the compound got so fed up of being called prostitutes that they formed an association and registered it as Bombay Sangeet Kalakar Mandal. They conducted interviews within the compound, speaking to singers, dancers, musicians, and compiled the list to present it to Prime Minister Indira Gandhi to declare them as artistes. Later, when she visited the actual Congress House building across the street, the tawaifs met her and thanked her for recognizing their work. They did not want to be clubbed with the flesh trade because that brought a lot of law and order problems with it. The tawaifs did not have to face those problems if they were established as artistes, who did not indulge in any illegal or criminal activities.

The compound was called Congress House because of its proximity to the Congress party's office situated close by. Many politicians and nationalists used to visit the kothas in the evening for a mujra performance. There was no hanky-panky involved; the kothas enjoyed their patronage and only much later, in its decline, did it become a hotbed of illicit activities. But throughout, it had to bear the indignity of being called a brothel where prostitutes lived because anything a woman does independently has always been read as her compromising her body. Walking through the dirty lane littered with garbage and paan stains, I saw a paan ki tapri, a paan shop.

Is this Congress House? I asked the paanwala.

Yes, go in, he said.

I walked in through the entrance of a building.

Could you please guide me to Ustad Noor Khan's house? I asked a young boy.

Who are you? he asked.

I am Rekha, from Calcutta, I said.

He said he had heard of me. This was a huge relief. He was Noor Khan's son. Noor Khan used to play the harmonium. He had performed with me in Calcutta. He had told me to meet him in Bombay if I ever visited the city. Noor Khan was in his fifties. He was sitting in a shaded area in the compound. He greeted me and called for tea. He heard me out and took me to Radha–Mala's kotha.

Radha–Mala were the most famous tawaif sisters in the compound at the time. Radha was a pretty performer. Mala was mostly a stage performer in private concerts outside the compound. They also had another sister, Bijli, but it was Radha–Mala who were the brilliant duo, sought even by film stars. They asked me about myself.

I want a room, I said.

Tum adhyaiy pe kar lo, said Radha. She was suggesting that I perform in her room and share the profits.

Nahi, didi, I said. Mujhe apna room chahiye. I want a room of my own.

She said there was an empty room in the building across hers in the compound. There were seven buildings in a circle in the compound, all filled with girls doing their business.

She spoke to someone and arranged to show me the room. The rent was fixed at four hundred rupees. I was not anxious to see the room, but went along anyway. I had seen so many similar, empty rooms in the past. It is what we make of an empty room that is more important. Not the room in itself. So I walked in and looked around, and approved of the tiny room without any questions. It had a small window opposite the door. The room opened out to a long balcony that led to other rooms. There was a common bathroom and a toilet at the end of the corridor.

I told Noor Khan to arrange for the gaddi and takiya, mattress and pillows. The seating arrangement was different in these quarters. When you opened the door, all three sides of the room were lined with thin, long gaddis propped with takiyas as backrest. The middle of the room was where the tawaifs sat singing and dancing. The music accompanists would have to sit behind her. So if you were arriving and happened to draw open the curtain of the room, you would watch a performance with the tawaif's back turned to you. She would also suspend a giant mirror above the window opposite the door to catch a glimpse of the party standing behind her, and would nod to them in the mirror. This way the performance remained uninterrupted and there was no room for anyone to step it, because the musicians were sitting close to the door with the shoes and sandals blocking the entrance.

I did not have much money, but I still managed to set up the room in less than a week of my arrival at Congress House. I had paid the rent in advance for a month. Noor Khan helped me procure the essentials. I went to the market and got a new set of ghungroos.

My neighbours were Uma on one side and Rajkumari on the other. There was a tall woman, Rashida, who lived on the ground floor with a manly woman. I found out much later that they were lovers. They were discreet, but since everyone knew about them, no one discussed it. All of them greeted me with warmth and struck a smile when they saw me. They were fascinated by my stories about Calcutta, as I was with their life in this big and bustling city of dreams. Everything I knew about Bombay was through films. It was always larger than life, and so also a little intimidating for a single woman. But since I had decided to land up there without any fear, I was not going to let it scare me. My new friends were impressed by my attitude. They had families in this business, so they did not have to step out of their comfort zone. You see, the bednis and deredaars, high-class courtesans, have a long history in the culture of the kotha. Raja-maharaja ke time se! From the time of royal patronage! They had roots. They did not have to struggle like me. They were not helpful to new competition. For a few days, no one came to my room. They were perhaps just watching me settle in. I had not yet called for you from Kalyan. My sister was taking care of you.

One day, Noor Khan took me to Akku aapa's room, which was on the ground floor. She was an old bai dressed in white. Her sons were musicians, her daughters were tawaifs. She was like an old guard of the compound, who had been there a long time and knew the history well. It was considered good to be social with her. We became instant friends. I liked her immediately. She had a kind face, a tactfully polite demeanour – like someone who had seen it all and could guide the young and new as a mentor. But since I had only just arrived, I stepped out less as I noticed that a lot of local rowdies roamed in the compound. Akku aapa often sent word for me, looking out for me. That made me feel comfortable and relaxed.

After two weeks, I returned to Kalyan and picked you up.

I do not know if I will be able to take care of him alone, I said to my sister.

She arranged for our stepbrother, a young man, dark in complexion had with empty eyes and a wiry body, to come along with me. His name was Ashok. He used to work in an orphanage. He was the son Tadiya had had with Gullo's sister, Shalu. It was the first time I was meeting him. Socho, just imagine, the child that Gullo wanted had grown up in an orphanage, and he was now going to take care of Gullo's daughter's child. Naseeb ka khel hai! It's a game of destiny! I said I would pay him, plus food and lodging. He agreed. We purchased utensils and a sigree, stove, with coal from the market. The room had an overhead loft with a staircase on the side of the door. We arranged to cook food in the day and use the loft as a resting area for him while my performance was under way at night.

A man named Shanti was one of the first patrons in Congress House. I sang the ghazals of Ghulam Ali: '*Hungama kyon hai barpa*', '*Yeh dil yeh paagal dil mera*', '*Chupke chupke raat din aansoon bahana yaad hai*'. I did not have much luck in my first few mujra mehfils. At midnight, a watchguard in the compound used to blow a whistle, and all the loiters and visitors would have to leave. He would then lock the gate. The rules of engagement were similar to Bandook Gully minus the whistle.

Noor Khan, whom I called Noor baba, told me about Foras Road, where the mujra mehfils went on till dawn.

Let us go to Foras Road, he said, seeing that my business was not picking up in Congress House.

Where is this road? I asked. What is there?

He told me about Bacchu Seth Ki Wadi. He told me about Iqbal aapa. She was a senior tawaif on her way out. She used to rent out her room to young girls, adhyay pe.

I will arrange a meeting with her, he said.

The next day, we went to meet her in the evening. I left you with Uma. Uma was thrilled to see you. She was a plump, mercurial character. She did not go to Foras Road as she did not need to – she had a steady flow of patrons. I was happy to leave you in her care. Ashok hung out with Pappu, Rajkumari's young son.

Noor baba and I took the back entrance, hired a taxi and landed up at Iqbal aapa's door. She was very welcoming, putting her hand on my head and blessing me. She was only seeing me as rent money, frankly. That evening, she introduced me to some patrons as 'Bow Bazaar ki mashoor naachnewali', the famous dancer of Bow Bazaar, Rekha. It would not sound like a pleasing introduction elsewhere, but, in the kothas, it is a matter of great pride to be called a famous naachnewali – after all, that is our dhanda.

I performed to a receptive crowd and took home good earnings for the night. I danced, and did my trademark step of bending over and picking up notes with my mouth. It excited them.

In Foras Road, the mujra culture was different. Here, anyone could walk in and walk out as we performed. There were no parties or group of men. It was called chhutta mujra. Small-change mujra. Men were free to walk into any room, watch for a while, pay the standard rate and leave. The standard rate was enough to get by on a daily basis. There was no need to transgress into anything else – like the flesh trade – if a tawaif decided to live off her daily earnings in this 'night shift'. Lots of young men came to watch a new girl with new dance tricks.

I think some of the songs I danced on were '*Tumko piya dil diya kitne naaz se*', '*Salaam-e-Ishq*', '*Chal dariya mein doob jaayein*' and '*Chhap tilak sab chhini re mose naina milaike*'.

Iqbal aapa loved my performance. I was thin, lean, tall and lithe. I was unlike most other women around, who were sitting around, and adding weight to their bodies and not to their performance. We shared the profits and I reached home at five in the morning. Sometimes, some of us girls got hungry after work, so we would go to the dhabas and five-star hotels in the Andheri suburbs. This cycle of performance continued for a while.

The deredaars, like my neighbour Uma, had a different mindset about performing at Foras Road. Since Congress House accommodated many old-timer gaanewalis, or gayikas, singers, who refused to modernize with the times and extend their hours like the new girls, they remained in a bubble – fading, dying. One could live in Congress House with a regular flow of patrons or do the 'night shift' in Foras Road for an additional cash flow to prepare for the future. The deredaarnis, in reality, had it both ways. The old gayikas stayed put in Congress House to give the impression that they were artistes, while someone from their family – or girls they had bought from elsewhere – toiled in Foras Road for them. I was doing both parts on my own, alone, because I was an outsider who wanted more from this life, from this profession. I had no lineage and no support network. I had to earn fast. I could not get complacent with the Congress House atmosphere.

The one thing in Congress House was that it was constantly under watch. If we heard the whistle at any hour, we understood that either someone had died or some event had occurred in the compound. The whistle was an alarm to signal 'tem bandh', or time up, for our work. There were days when we heard it in the middle of the day. It meant a day off for us. We used the rest of the day to go visit Chowpatty beach, and eat golgappas and chuskis. We let the sea breeze caress our hair and salt our talk.

The first thing I used to do after returning from Foras Road at five in the morning was fill buckets of water and store them in the room or outside my gate. Water was released only at certain hours for a limited period. There was a common water tap on the floor, where the tawaifs or their servants would gather in the mornings. Sleepy and tired, everyone operated in silence or in low, exhausted voices at that time of the day. Seeing tawaifs unpainted, drowsy and quiet was like looking at their sad souls walking around in a daze. The act of filling water in the morning was enough to ground me to the reality of my life. It was filled with the hardship of a daily routine to survive, while working as a glamourous performer all night. It was easy to dream that some man would want me so much that he would whisk me away from this drudgery and I would live like a queen. One splash of cool water in the misty morning light not only removed the layers of make-up I wore, but also woke me up to the reality of my situation.

I used to sleep next to you on the floor and wake up by mid-afternoon. By three, I would prepare the food. Ashok had been trained to change your nappies and feed you when I slept. This arrangement worked well without interruption.

Between three and nine in the night, when Congress House buzzed with mujras, I had enough time to manage you and my daily riyaaz, along with visits to the market or the salon. I used to wear sarees for all activities.

What a silly girl to bind yourself in a saree all day, pagal ladki, Akku aapa taunted me one day.

She said the most thoughtful things in the least compassionate tone. It did not sound rude, just practical.

Salwar-kurta sila le, she said. Get a salwar-kurta stitched.

On her insistence, I got three sets stitched – one in a badami, almond, colour, another in sky blue and one more in a colour I am forgetting now. The first two were in silk, the third in cotton.

When I wore it, I felt so liberated. She was right. I thanked Akku aapa and told her, I can do more in these. She laughed and teased me, saying, I told you so. Her knees had given in to old age; she was almost immobile now, sitting in one corner of her room. Salwars had given her the freedom to move; sarees would have mummified her.

But the salwar-kurta was a daytime casual outfit. We could not wear it in the mujras. I had not seen anyone do it. In the evening, we had to pull out our best sarees and gussy up for the best night of someone else's life.

Iqbal aapa favoured me over the other girls because I brought something new to the mujra that the local girls were not able to – the grit to excel. I met the sarangi player Ustad Sultan Khan again in Bombay.

Arre, Rekha, tu? You? He was surprised to see me in Congress House.

We joked about the past. I invited him home. Uma, my neighbour, was also a good dancer. She had featured as a dancer in the film *Chitralekha*. I think she was in the song '*Maara gaya brahmachari*' with Mehmood.

Khair, when she saw Khan saab visiting me, she started acting shy around him. She was known to have a reputation as an unpredictable, moody, snappy deredaar – an entitled one, no less. She used to think highly of herself. She was always making faces and reacting sharply to conversations. I was becoming wary of her. I would spend less time in her room.

When she started cosying up to Khan saab, I was more than happy for her. She was older, did not go to Foras Road and was desperately looking for a man after her failed romances with a few locals, including Paape, who had limited her freedom. I think Khan saab married her, or 'kept' her – I am not sure what happened to her after I left Bombay. Akku aapa told me that alcohol killed Uma a few years later. So many women were like her. Manju, another beautiful woman, also had a similar fate with another musician. Thank god I did not ruin my life for a tabalchi, tabla player!

I was friends with Putli, a young bai my age. Putli had a patron named Adnan. He used to take women from the kothas to stand or perform as extras in Hindi films. Putli was star-struck. She was hopeful that a famous director would discover her. She was a bit plump, had teeth jutting out and considered her dark skin a curse.

Safed powder pott leti thi mooh par. Putli used to cake her face with white powder.

We were as thick as thieves at one point in time. Adnan took us to Grant Road station and from there we travelled by train to a film studio to watch a shoot. The film was *Aap Toh Aise Na The*. Actors Raj Babbar, Ranjeeta Kaur and Tamanna were filming a song sequence in a party.

We used to get a hundred and twenty-five rupees for acting as extras. Adnan used to deduct a commission of twenty-five rupees. It was good money to do nothing. We were provided food and it was a great way for the girls to hang out together. We went infrequently, depending on our availability, because these shoots used to take an entire day.

We used to ask Adnan who the star was. That is how we went to see Padmini Kolhapure in *Zamaane Ko Dikhana Hai*, Rishi Kapoor in *Karz*, Jeetendra and Tina Munim in *Deedar-e-Yaar*, Manoj Kumar in *Kranti*, Zeenat Aman in *Pakhandi* and Anil Kapoor in *Mashaal*. We saw Amitabh Bachchan, Shatrughan Sinha and Jackie Shroff at the *Kaalia* premiere. We also saw Rekha, Dharmendra, Hema Malini, Mithun, Reena Roy Kaur and so many more. I was in a song with Asha Sachdev and Deepak Parashar, which was shot in Malad.

Tina Munim was rude to us junior artistes. She did not meet us warmly. She had big airs about her. Zeenat Aman was so lovely. She had the best body, a dancer's body. Some of us girls barged into her dressing room. She spoke to us.

How was my dance? she asked.

We told her how fabulous she was. She laughed, smoking a cigarette. She looked even more beautiful when she laughed.

Where are you girls from? she asked.

Congress House, one of us said. I was too star-struck to say a word. I was not educated, so I used to be shy around film stars and not open my mouth.

Oh, then I should say I was okay. You girls are the real dancers, she said.

She made us feel so comfortable.

Shabana Azmi came with Farooq Shaikh to meet Radha–Mala to observe them for her role in *Mandi*. I met them then. Once, I saw Lata Mangeshkar getting out of her Pedder Road apartment. I was walking on the other side of the road. A patron, who had invited me to his flat to perform, was walking with me.

Look, that is Lata, he said.

I wanted to run across the street, touch her feet and hug her and call her didi. Her songs meant so much to me. I was fond of Mohammad Rafi's voice too. When he was in the Bombay Hospital after he had suffered a heart attack, I reached there with some bais. We were told that he had died. I sobbed for him. I really liked him a lot.

I wanted to meet Helen desperately. She was my guru. My appreciation of the performing arts came from watching her and Vyjayanthimala dance. '*Muqabla hum se na karo*' was my favourite dance number and it featured both of them. In the dance face-off, the legendary fleet-footed actresses express themselves with such flair and joy – kya thirakti thi! I had learnt so much just by watching this sequence. The lyrics of the song resonated with my own struggle: Do not compete with me, they sang, I am trying to be the best version of myself.

I had met Saroj Khan when she was showing Shoma Anand how to dance in *Patita*. At that time, Saroj Khan had not achieved the fame that she would reach with Sridevi and Madhuri. But it was still unusual – and a moment of pride for us – to see another woman choreographing a song sequence in an all-male film-crew environment.

Choreographer Bulbul once picked me to be part of his troupe for a song. Rekha was dancing in a film set designed to look like a kabila, a tribal village. I was selected to dance in the crowd.

Bulbul would tell me to shake my hands up in the air, and that is all I remember of that song. I was so star-struck to see Rekha in real life. I did not approach her, maybe because I was so raw on film sets. I never saw the song in any of her films, but I do remember she was wearing a green dress and dancing.

Sometimes, film people would put us girls in a separate room and ask us to dance. Someone said light on, someone said camera roll, and someone said action. Then someone said music. Then someone played music. We danced. People watched. I am quite sure now that the camera was not on. It was a scam. I did not see myself on-screen in any of those shady films. But we were paid for it, so we didn't bother.

Malkhan, a scheming chap who worked as a cab driver at the Bombay airport, also began to take us to shoots.

One day, he said to me, Rekha, there is a special sequence in Shanmukhananda Hall. I want you to meet some important film people. Dress classy.

I wore a blue chiffon saree. I still have it.

I met some producers and directors. I did not know who they were. Must have been some small-timers.

Malkhan said they wanted to take my pictures. So someone did that. Then, actor Mukesh Khanna walked in with a briefcase and fought with some goons – that was the scene. The film was called 'Revenge' at the time. I am quite sure it was never made.

Revenge toh mujhe lena chahiye tha Malkhan se! I should have taken revenge on Malkhan. I could not sense that he was an impostor when he asked me for money for a song recording. I gave it to him because I was told I had a part in the film. I was going to play a bhootni, a ghost, who walks with a candle and sings a woeful tune. In those days, bhoot films were a rage.

I gave him some five or eight thousand rupees, because I thought I was going to be a heroine. We shot the sequence for a day. I was convinced. I wore a white saree and walked with a burning candle in a jungle. The scene was shot at dusk in some studio. Fog was generated from a machine. The whole thing looked professional.

Lata Mangeshkar has sung the song for your sequence, he said.

He made me listen to a song on a tape recorder. I think it was the song '*Badi der ki meherbaan aate aate*'. I was thrilled. It was more than I had ever hoped for. Lata didi! She was singing for me! Mere toh paseene chhut gaye! I was breaking out in a sweat.

Then Malkhan said the film would take some time to release. He said a director was considering me for the main lead in *Roohi*. He wanted more money. Reluctantly, I gave him some more. I was also being greedy in the hope of a role. Then I did not see Malkhan for months. Cheating-baaz he was. The girls in the kotha said all of them had been a heroine for a day on a film set. We are heroines of this place every day. Why waste your time there? That made sense.

Dhurr, I said, who wants to get into this when I saw that my money was only going, not coming. After that, I stopped thinking about films and concentrated on my mujras. There were so many famous bais languishing – how was my naseeb going to shine?

The famous Mubarak Begum, who sang so many beautiful melodies in films, like '*Mujhko apne gale laga lo*' and '*Kabhi tanhaiyon mein*', also lived in Congress House. In my early days in the compound, Mubarak Begum came to collect chanda for the tawaif committee. She stood at my door and said, Mera naam Mubarak Begum hai. My name is Mubarak Begum. She must have been around forty-five years of age then. Rajkumari and Uma were giving her eleven rupees each, so I did the same. At that moment, it had not struck me that it was the same Mubarak Begum who sang in films. I thought, Hogi koi apne zamaane ki mashoor baiji. Must have been some popular courtesan of her time. I had heard her songs on the radio. I had not seen her photograph. It was only much later that I found out that she was the singer the Mangeshkar sisters kept out of the competition. She was languishing here. But she also moved out soon. Many years later, I saw in the news on television that she had died in Jogeshwari, languishing in poverty.

Naseem Chopra, who sang '*Dekh toh dil ke jaan se uthta hai*' in *Pakeezah* was here as well. The nautch girl who danced in the song '*Jalta hai badan*' in *Razia Sultan* was from here. They were not getting work. Begum Akhtar was said to have come here to meet her friends in the early seventies. I heard she even performed with the bade ustads here. Ustad Alla Rakha played here. Ghulam Ali sang here as well as in Bandook Gully. I also met Chhoti Akhtar in Bacchu Seth Ki Wadi. She used to imitate Begum Akhtar. She had a daughter who was launched as Deepa in a film called *Madhavi* with Sanjay Khan. Deepa did not do another film. I do not know what happened to her, but it was rumoured that Chhoti Akhtar killed herself by jumping off the Gateway of India. I heard the fractious mother–daughter relationship was the tipping point.

It was also rumoured that Dilip Kumar had seen Nimmi perform here. It is said he had seen Madhubala here. Once, an ustad took me to Chamiyan bai's house. She was Saira Banu's grandmother.[1]

---

1   Shaheen Raaj, 'Nostalgia: Saira Banu', Nasheman.in, 29 August 2017, https://nasheman.in/nostalgia-saira-banu/#:~:text=Her%20maternal%20grandmother%20was%20the,daughter%20of%20her%20brother%20Sultan; Saira Banu, 'Wake Up Every Day Feeling Robbed: Saira Banu Pens Exclusive Tribute for Dilip Kumar on News18 Showsha', News18, 7 July 2022, https://www.news18.com/news/movies/wake-up-every-morning-feeling-robbed-saira-banu-pens-exclusive-tribute-for-dilip-kumar-on-news18-showsha-5504329.html; Seema Sonik Alimchand, *Jubilee Kumar: The Life and Times of a Superstar*, Hachette India, 2020, https://books.google.co.in/books?id=ym_ODwAAQBAJ&pg=PT175&lpg=PT175&dq=chamiyan+bai+saira+banu+grandmother&source=bl&ots=cNvR2C6V6s&sig=ACfU3U0yU0PA6QmW_DzNgLoVYgh_P4CkXQ&hl=en&sa=X&ved=2ahUKEwj_2J_Y0-78AhW7zqACHfasArc4FBDoAXoECBUQAw#v=onepage&q=chamiyan%20bai%20saira%20banu%20grandmother&f=false

I thought I might catch a glimpse of Dilip Kumar – issi bahane se at least I would get to see him – but I had no such luck.

In those days, Dhoraji, a small town in Gujarat, used to host an annual mela on the precincts of a dargah. Girls from Congress House would go there to perform in tents.

Once, an organizer, Chaman Bapu, said, Rekha, you also come this time.

No, I said. I had heard stories of how arduous it was. I did not want to put myself through that grind.

You can earn twenty-five thousand in ten days, he said.

My eyes opened wide. That was a lot of money in those days.

But how will I go? I have a small child with me, I said.

Think about it, was his response.

I called my sister Babbo and told her, You stay here and look after my child. I will return in ten days.

I had never done an outstation show before in this city. In Bombay, we used to get calls for shows in hotel rooms, small venues, annual day functions. Those were safe spaces because we usually went in groups.

This was the first time I was going to be alone, performing solo, in my own tent show. Chaman Bapu said he would arrange everything. He was a regular patron. I trusted him. He only chose the best dancers in the business for this golden opportunity.

The tent was called Chaman Bapu Tent. Soda bottles were sold inside. Banta soda. The tent could accommodate quite a crowd. Girls used to come from different cities to perform in various other tents. The tents had special stage-performance names like Phool Tent, Kaanch Tent, Phirki Tent.

Phirki! I asked Chaman if I could have the same name. 'O phirkiwali, kal phir aana,' I recalled the song from my childhood.

He said it would create confusion. Now if someone already had the name, I had to get a new one too.

So what, then, should my name be?

Tum toh Bijli ho, he announced with a jubilant laugh.

Bijli. Lightning.

He said my moves were as quick as lightning.

I did not argue. I had to be faster than Phirki. I was ready to compete.

A group of musicians accompanied me. The performance would usually start with a dance in the evening after sunset, around eight.

We would warm up to the tune of '*O lal meri pat rakhiyo bala jhule laalan*'. This was a percussion-heavy qawwali that could be improvised according to its reception. It gave the troupe time to assemble a crowd, and, once they had packed in as many people as they could, I would get up and dance, instructing the musicians to increase the tempo and follow my rhythm.

At its peak, when the crowd would begin to jive, the song turned into a frenzy – the claps, the vocals, the dance, all soaring to a feverish pitch. It could either crack at its zenith or splinter through the skies.

Those days two-rupee and five-rupee notes were widely circulated. Young men came from all over Gujarat – Junagadh, Porbandar, Surat, Ahmedabad – showering notes on us.

Manchale, the randy public was. Loud, rambunctious.

In five days, the name of the marquee had to be changed to Bijli Tent. '*Damadam mast qalandar*' made me a star attraction – I would dance on the hot sands in a ghagra, almost running a temperature in the heat. I do not know what got into me. I was unstoppable.

Part of me was a performer and part of me became a jogan. I twirled and twirled, doing the spin and the chakkar on my knees. In kathak, I had learnt to spin a hundred times.

Chaman Bapu watched me in awe and horror.

You have too much willpower, he said.

A favourite melody of mine at that time was '*Nikla hai gora gora chand re sajanwa kar ke jatan koi aaja*'.

Men kept streaming into the tent, and, at one point, the audience turned into a roaring mob. I was scared that the crowd would get rowdy any minute. Chaman Bapu had understood this much before me. He controlled the crowd by constantly talking to them to distract them. He claimed that he was carrying a pistol and waved a stick in the air to frighten the men, saying he would fire his gun to disperse them if they did not behave. The trick worked. Those were ten gruelling days of daily performances all night long. When we saw the first rays of the sun hitting the tent, we knew it was time to slow down. People would not leave otherwise. Lecherous men would follow us to our rooms, stalking us. After sharing profits with the musicians, I made about fifteen thousand rupees.

The next year, when Chaman Bapu asked me to go, I said it was too demanding. I did not want to go through ten nights of dancing. He told me to take someone along this time. I took Akku aapa and Putli. Although I did most of the work, having them there with me made me feel safer. I could take breaks during the performance. Akku aapa would sing and Putli filled in when I was taking a breather behind the tent.

I made more money in the second year. Ours was the most visited tent. I did it for one more year.

There were these raucous admirers in the tents on the one hand, and on the other were the sheikhs who came from the sands to our kothas. Sheikhs from Dubai used to visit Foras Road in groups, but not so frequently. When they came, the girls had to be in top form. They used to fill the room with cash. God alone knows how much they understood, but they showered the girls in currency notes of all denominations, starting with one rupee and going up to ten rupees. Maybe they came directly from an exchange counter. About seven of us – including Tanu, Shabana, Putli and I – used to perform in

Foras Road. We used to often leave from Congress House at the same time after the whistle went off.

That is how I met Mohammad Qamar. He was sitting with his sheikh friends in Iqbal aapa's room. He was fair and tall, and had a combed moustache; he wore a safari suit, a gold watch and shiny shoes. He looked royal. He was the only one in his group who spoke Hindi to some degree. When I first met him, they were listening to someone singing. I waited outside for my turn. Iqbal aapa introduced me to the party. She was sitting next to Qamar when she gestured to me and called me in.

Qamar saab, yeh ladki kya khoob naachti hai, she said. She is a fantastic dancer.

He understood what she meant, while the others nodded as if they, too, followed what had been said.

'*Piya tose naina laage re*' pe iska dance dekhiye, she said. Watch her dance to '*Piya tose naina laage re*'.

He looked at me as the others nodded. Qamar was fond of old classical songs.

I wore my ghungroos, reading their faces. I could see that they were not prepared to see this ordinary and thin girl perform.

I had worn a simple maroon saree that day with minimal make-up and no shiny ornaments, except for jhumkas and bangles.

I instructed the ustads and two girls to sit and sing along with me. When I snapped a note from Qamar's hand with my trademark move, he was stunned. I saw that he had taken an instant liking to me. His eyes did not blink. He did not want to miss a beat, a turn of the hip, a coquettish smile of an adaakara, performer. My nazakat, finesse, was not tempered by artful expressions, but by quicksilver moves to thrill. Money filled the room that night; notes began flying around as if in a dream sequence. I did not know if I should be happy and continue dancing or if I should stop, but the shower of notes only accelerated my performance, shining through it. After the performance, Noor baba was the happiest.

Subhanallah, aaj toh beta tu ne kamaal kar diya, he said, patting my back and saying that I had performed wonderfully that night. Although he treated me like his daughter, he used the word beta, son, to address me because, to him, I was no less than a man. I did not mind being called a man in a man's world. I guess as a provider for my family, I was doing what was expected of a man and so that gave me the feeling that I was equal to one.

Noor baba had become my guru. We did not have a gadhbandha – the ritual thread-tying ceremony where a teacher wraps a sacred thread on the disciple's wrist to formalize their lifelong association as musicians – but we bonded like guru and shishya. I gave him more than the usual cut, not because he congratulated me, but because we had made a lot as a team that night.

Iqbal aapa was in tears. I will not take extra, she said, when I tried to give her a fair share. You deserve more, she told me.

The next day, the same group of men was waiting for me. I sang a few ghazals this time. Qamar got a chance to watch me closely. I do not know what it was about me that enchanted him. For the next couple of days, Qamar requested that only I sing and dance for him. He was not keen on the other girls, although he did not mind them as part of the chorus, and paid them as well.

One night, after we had wrapped up our gig, Qamar asked me, Resha, tum kahan rehti ho? Where do you live? He pronounced my name with an 's' instead of a 'k'. He had a funny accent when he spoke Hindi. You come here at midnight and disappear before dawn, he said.

He made it sound like I was a character in a fairy tale. I laughed and tried to avoid replying to him.

One of the rules of engagement in Foras Road was to never talk about private matters to patrons. Iqbal aapa had warned us to never reveal where we lived. But since I was her favourite, she had been using me as bait to seduce the sheikh party every night.

She lives in Congress House, Iqbal aapa herself piped up.

That must have burst his bubble about me. What had she blurted out? She had broken her own rule. It was her affection for me that had made her speak up. She must have thought it was a harmless admission. Or she must have thought it through – the sheikh party was not going to suddenly shift their entertainment programme to Congress House, where the mujras ceased at twelve. That was when fairy princesses like us stepped out of our dreary castles to look for new punters.

I am leaving for Muscat tomorrow, he said.

Iqbal aapa must have breathed a sigh of relief when I did not react.

Theek hai, I said.

I did not act like a tart. Anyone else would have said how she was going to miss him. Men love being repeatedly told how much their absence torments us women. I had no such delusions. I had seen what men had done to my trust in the past. I was not there to snag myself another one. Qamar simply smiled and left.

Iqbal aapa rushed to me and said, Hai, kuch toh atka ke rakhti usse! You should have kept him on a hook.

After a few months, when Qamar returned, he was at my door in Congress House. He came directly from the airport. It was around four in the evening. Our doors are usually open and I saw his silhouette in the light streaming in from outside.

Arre aap, I said. Aaiye, baithiye. Please sit.

Mine was not the best-decorated room. It was small and shabby. I was in an unkempt state myself and was not ready to face a patron just then. I did not know what impression he would have had of me.

You live here, he said. Then he spotted you and exclaimed, Who is this?

My son, I said.

Your son? He was shocked.

He was not expecting to see me – a young girl he thought was barely out of her teens – with a child.

And who is this? he asked, looking at Ashok sitting in one corner, as if to fully absorb what he had heard and to confirm if the man in the room had anything to do with it.

My brother, I said.

The smile returned to his face. I think he was trying to understand how a fair, beautiful boy like you could be that man's child.

Reassured – though he still didn't know who the father was – his voice filled with astonishment.

Hain, yeh tumhara ladka hai? Is he your son? he said. Bahut khoobsurat hai. He's beautiful.

He immediately picked you up for a hug. In that moment, in that fleeting but indelible moment, with both of you cheek to cheek, he looked like the father of my child. Both of you had the same fair complexion, round features and big, beautiful eyes. I had to lower my own eyes in embarrassment and smile. He could have been your father. He would have made a better father than anyone else.

Qamar was a refined man from high-society Muscat. He worked for the government. He was soft-spoken, cheerful and polite. He exuded good manners and grace. Impeccably dressed in the finest-looking shirts and trousers, with perfectly combed hair and beard, he was the gentleman I hoped my child would become. I sent Ashok to fetch a soft drink from the compound. Qamar did not wait for it.

I have to go now, he said.

He put some money in your hand. It was a lot. Some five or six hundred rupees, I think. You clasped and crumpled the crisp notes as if it were a new paper toy. He left. I wrested the notes from your tight grip and straightened them out. They smelt of him. Class.

The next day, Iqbal aapa got news of his return. I did not turn up at Foras Road, though. Iqbal aapa, who rarely stepped out of her residence, came to see me.

What happened, Rekha? Why are you not coming to my place for the past two days? she asked.

My child has not been well, I said.

Let us go to Haji Ali, she said. And pray for your child's good health.

We walked behind the dargah, looking out at the sea, watching waves crash and talking frankly about Qamar.

Did he come? she asked.

Yes, I said.

Did he see your son? she asked.

Yes, I said. When he walked in, I was holding my son in my arms.

You know, he has two daughters. He wants a son, she said.

I did not understand what she was implying, but I could sense it was not good news.

He is a very good man, she said. But see how it goes. Be careful, she advised.

When was a tawaif not to be careful? It was the kind of advice we could toss away with the waves.

Just remember one thing – he hates people who chew on paan. He finds it vulgar to spit in public, she said.

We laughed and drank sherbets outside the dargah. We were both addicted to paan.

Qamar arrived the next day with Iqbal aapa. The four of us, including you, went to the five-star Taj Hotel for dinner. I was not used to going out to fancy places, so he had bought me an elegant silk saree and pearls to wear. He bought clothes for you as well.

The four of us behaved like a family, ate quietly and spoke even more softly, as if someone would find out our secret. I did not even know how to look at the menu. Qamar made me feel relaxed.

When we stepped out in the humid air after a lovely, cool evening inside the hotel, Qamar pulled out a packet from his pockets. He had been carrying a paan for me all this while.

Resha, paan khayegi? Will you have a paan? he asked on Marine Drive, where we were sauntering.

Both Iqbal aapa and I had a hearty laugh. He was such a thoughtful man. Iqbal aapa and I shared the paan. He dropped us home.

Qamar became a regular patron. He took us out to the Taj, the Oberoi, Bombay International Hotel, the Intercontinental and many other five-star hotels and restaurants around Marine Drive for dinner. He spent lavishly on us, buying us clothes, accessories, perfumes, shoes and jewellery – and choosnis, pacifiers, and milk bottles for you. He pampered you a lot.

Once, he showed me his suite in a towering hotel. It was so beautiful that I cried. I could not believe my luck. We used to work so hard in such small rooms, and here I was, sitting like a queen in a grand room filled with flowers and drapes. I felt so thankful that life had shown me such wonderful sights. I could look out of the window and watch the sea. I felt so blessed.

Another time, when we were dining at the Ambassador Hotel's revolving restaurant, it felt like we were in a mela. The tables were moving; I found it funny and silly, but enjoyed it, feeling slightly dizzy. I was in the same room where my favourite actor, Manoj Kumar, had shot the song 'Bharat ka rehnewala hoon' in the film Purab Aur Pachhim. Qamar hummed the tune and reminded me of it. But I laughed and told him it felt all so foreign in there.

I used to be afraid of going to big places because my manners were still small, but he would make me feel comfortable by asking a friend of mine or Ashok to join us. And he made sure you were always with us.

I stopped going to Foras Road entirely. Iqbal aapa was upset.

See, aapa, I come to your place to dance, not to mix with the patrons. I cannot stop him from coming to Congress House. If he is expecting more from me, then he needs to be clear about it. I am not like the girls in Foras Road, who do both businesses there, I explained to her.

She understood what I meant. I was not selling sex. She calmed down. She knew that she could not strain her relationship with me as once this Qamar chapter ended, I would return to her room to dance.

I saw many film personalities in these hotels where we went to for dinner. I saw Sharmila Tagore at the upscale Copper Chimney restaurant. Raj Kumar, Jalal Agha, Heena Kausar – filmmaker K. Asif's daughter, who married the gangster Iqbal Mirchi – Runa Laila, and so many others. I saw them all in various hotels and restaurants across the city. In those days, the silk and chiffon sarees that Zeenat Aman wore in the film *Dostana* were quite popular. I had a range of those in yellow, blue and pink. I used to wear them often when I went out. Uma, my neighbour, also borrowed them from me. Qamar used to spend a lot on us. The scent of money and class is heady, but I was not addicted to it. I knew my reality.

Why don't you and your son shift with me to Muscat? Qamar finally said it one day. Marry me.

But you are already married, I pointed out.

Yes, but we can live together, he said.

His intentions became very clear. Be careful, Iqbal aapa had said earlier. Now her words stung in my ears.

I cannot do that, I said. I cannot share my child with others. We belong here – this is where our home is.

I do not know what came over me in that moment. I feared that he would take me to a foreign country, and dump me or separate me from you. I was constantly worried that someone or the other was trying to take my child away from me. Your father had tried once already.

We cannot go, I said, tearing the passports he had made for us. That was the end of Qamar.

I began to worry for your safety because something or the other kept happening around you. People wanted to either adopt you or some incident would tear you away from my sight, triggering morbid fears inside me. Once, on Independence Day, I returned from Dhoraji after a dance programme. I sent you out with Ashok for a walk. My feet were swollen that day. I wanted to sleep. He took you to the beach, but as the hours passed, you two didn't return. I grew anxious and went running around the compound looking for you. What happened to Ashok? Where was he? Why was he taking so long to bring you back? Had he lost you? I became paranoid. When he returned, I slapped him.

Where were you? I asked.

I was watching a film on the beach, he said.

In those days, the public could watch films on open screens set up on the beach. Ashok would often go to the beach to watch a film. I had to be careful because he could get so engaged in the film that he could lose sight of you playing in the sand nearby. What if someone took you away then?

Another time, I hired a servant named Salim. You were about two years old at the time. I used to leave you with Ashok and go to perform in Foras Road. Once, he asked Salim to fetch him a tablet for a headache. Salim gave him a sleeping pill. When I returned, I saw that the front gate was open, but Ashok had locked the door to the main room, where he was now lying unconscious. You were sleeping next to him. I found it unusual that the front gate was open in the wee hours. I banged hard on the door.

Ashok! I cried. Open the door!

He did not respond. I tried a few more times. There was no sound from inside the room. I peeped through the keyhole. It was dark inside. I could hear a faint rumbling. You heard my voice. You crawled towards the door. You began crying. I thought something terrible had happened. Neighbours, who had gathered around by then, suggested I break open the door.

But if we break the door, my child will be hurt, I said. He is standing at the door.

I started telling you to move away from the door.

Beta, move, move; go back, go back. I am coming in. Step back, step back, I said repeatedly.

It took a while for you to understand and move away from the door. When you had moved towards the far end of the room, I told one of the men gathered to break open the door. He kicked it a few times and slammed his shoulder against it. After a few attempts, he managed to break in.

Ashok was lying unconscious. I ran to you and calmed you down. Someone tried to wake Ashok, but he was not stirring. Salim had returned by this time. I asked him what had happened. He said he did not know anything. All he had done was fetch a pill for Ashok's headache.

After a few hours, when Ashok woke up, he told me in a few words what had happened. He spoke less, but always told the truth. I suspected foul play from Salim and sent him away. I then hired a girl, Kookie, to look after you. She would carry you around the compound, taking you to the kothas all evening. Celebrities, artistes and film stars in attendance would ask her whose child it was. She would act shy. They would give her money. She did it often, until I heard of it. One time actor Ajit Khan said, Bada pyaara baccha hai, what a cute child, and asked to adopt you.

So you carry my son around to earn money? I asked her.

No, no, she said, only rich people think like that. I do not ask for the money.

I forbade her from taking you out in the evenings.

Then I got Hasina. When she was a teenager, her parents sold her off to the bednis. She was my cousin sister. When I was in Calcutta, she was in Ramkali ki baari. Back then, I was staying in ekyasi number. I did not meet her in Calcutta because of her notoriety with men. The bednis were training her in the arts, but she was slow to learn. She was fair, beautiful and tall, so talent did not matter. She got by on her looks alone.

She started frequenting the Race Course grounds in Calcutta after a man, Abid Mirza, fell in love with her. She started wearing silk sarees and dark sunglasses, carrying a fancy purse and strutting around in high heels. She enjoyed the thrills of watching the game with Mirza, who bred horses for the race, was a punter and known to be a rich man with a refined taste for the good things in life. She thought she was the good thing in his life: his mistress. She felt she was part of high society, lunching with the ladies at Race Course and pretending to be Mirza's wife.

I met Mirza once. He had come to Bandook Gully for my performance. He was a short, bald man, but was still handsome. Mirza had christened her Hasina – her real name was Reema. Soon, the jockeys were getting a good look at their new owner. She would visit them in the stables and strike up a friendship. Mirza did not like her proximity to one particular man. The jockey whisked her away to Bombay, promising her a better arena – the Mahalaxmi Racecourse, where the film stars hobnobbed.

After a few years, she was done with the jockey. Rather, he dumped her. She could not return to Calcutta. Who would take her back? She was so indecisive. She went to her brother Raju's house in a slum in Yerawada. She stayed with him, doing nothing.

When I shifted to Congress House, she heard about me from our relatives who lived in Yerawada. She went to meet my jijaji, Anoop, in Kalyan, to plead with him to take her to me. She wanted to return to this life. She did not know how to make her way back into it. Till then, she did not even know about Congress House.

Anoop jijaji came to me and said, Reema wants to stay with you.

No, no, I said, I have heard stories about her; I do not want her around. She is trouble.

He told her the truth. She insisted that she had learnt her lesson. She came to meet me with him.

Please keep me with you, she pleaded.

No, I said, you do not know how to sing and dance. What will you do here?

I will learn; I will look after your child, she said.

I saw that she was indeed beautiful, but there was also something rough about her edges. She could be polished. I was having trouble with finding someone to look after you. I could not rely entirely on Ashok. A woman would be better to have around, and someone from my distant family suited me. It was a win-win situation for me. She was not going to be competition in performance, which I was sure of.

Ek se do bhala, I said to myself and took her in. Two helping hands are better than one.

All right, I said to my jijaji, leave her here.

I dressed her in the best clothes and make-up, and asked her to sit on the side during my performance. Usually, three or four girls would sit in a room on one side, watching a performance and singing along when the performer stood up to dance. Hasina was relegated to the duty of a chorus girl.

You sing and learn from me first, I said.

She did as she was told.

When I went out to perform in venues or hotel rooms, she was at home with Ashok to look after you. Ashok also got a chance to step out and hang out with the boys. Hasina began to befriend the women in the compound, watching and learning, observing and making her own friends. She was quite active and smart.

After I returned from my performance, I would find her dressed in the best of sarees, her thick black hair tied in the trendiest of hairdos. She had a lot of time on her hands, sitting in the room and fashioning new looks for herself, but without an audience. She was grooming herself for a rich man. We got along well. I did not mind her around, as she took the best care of you – perhaps she saw you as a toy to help her bide her time till the right man walked in.

There were rumours that she was flirting with a few roadside romeos, but nothing that I saw. I had not yet taken her to Foras Road. I did not think she was ready. I had tried sitting with her on riyaaz for song and dance. She had the looks, but no talent.

In those days, a tall, unattractive but charming goonda Niyaaz was after my life. I knew him from Calcutta. He used to bother me in Bandook Gully, but only with his words when he got drunk and filled with lust. He would write my name along with his on the wall using a lipstick, a piece of charcoal, a pen – anything he could find to deface the kotha with his obsessive proclamations of true love. He did not carry knives and guns on him. I was scared of weapons, but I also knew facing my fears made me more courageous, and the writing on the wall was the easiest to get rid of. Niyaaz was from Rajasthan. He was also a petty train robber. He would tell me stories of his escapes to Nepal when things got hot. He once robbed a goods train full of clothes. He called me to Minerva Hotel, behind the Bandook Gully kotha, and asked me to take as many sarees as I wanted. Now, why to lie, he told me he had stolen them. Some sarees were very good. I took a few. He asked me to travel to Jaipur with him and settle down. I said I would give it a thought. I kept him on the hook for a few years until I came to Bombay. He followed me there.

One afternoon, when he landed up at my kotha, I was surprised. He insisted I accompany him. Do not bother me, I said. I have to go to see my sister in Ambernath. I picked you up and tried to look busy. Niyaaz grabbed my hand, broke a red glass bangle on my wrist and said, I will eat this bangle if you try to leave.

Are you mad or what? I asked. I was irritated. He put the bangle inside his mouth and started chewing on it. I could hear the sound of glass crunching against his teeth. Love made him do these crazy things. Hasina walked in at that moment and watched him.

She liked such men. Who is she? Niyaaz asked with a bruised, bloody mouth. Hasina giggled. It was love at first sight for them.

Niyaaz and Hasina started seeing each other. I did not mind them together. He had a good heart. What I did not foresee was how Hasina would suck him dry and move on to the next maaldaar, loaded, party. Soon, she got bored of him and began eyeing other goons in the compound. She would pit one goon against another and wait for the worst one to win her hand. Niyaaz went back to his village and never returned.

Once, I was invited to perform in a flat in Nariman Point. The bais used to go to perform for goons like Ganesh, Manzoor and a few other names I am forgetting now. These guys were proper goondas with guns. Hasina had befriended Putli by then. She told Putli to convince me to take her along.

Yaar, she does not know anything, I told Putli. Phans jayenge. We'll get stuck.

Nothing will happen, she said. I am there. I will keep her by my side.

Why even take her to sit? I asked. What is the point?

Arre yaar, said Putli, let her have some fun. She has been sitting here doing nothing all this time.

Hasina pretended she did not know what was going on. She was aware when we got gigs to perform for goondas. She wanted to see them. Maybe she was actively seeking them out. I was too naïve to understand her intentions. She spoke less, and acted quiet and coy around me. I felt bad that I was not allowing her to have a good time. So we dressed her up and took her along with us. When we reached the flat, there were other bais as well. Nargis, Manju and a few other girls were already lined up to perform. I got a turn at four in the morning. By that time, these accomplished bais had performed well and emptied all the pockets.

What will you get now? asked one ustad.

I was nervous, and thought that after one dance act they would wind up and we would get nothing. But I danced with all my heart, even balancing a bottle of alcohol on my head at one point. Some small-time film actors were in the audience as well. I do not know their names, but I have seen them in side roles in the films of Rajesh Khanna and Dharmendra. One goonda, Ganesh, was eyeing Hasina while I performed.

Didi, he said to me, ask her to dance.

I took him into confidence and whispered in his ear, Bhai saab, she is learning, she is not ready yet.

I thought I had managed to save the situation. However, had I allowed it, maybe what happened next would not have taken place. When Ganesh realized that she was new and fresh, his interest in her grew even more. These guys love a new baby doll. So what if she cannot perform? She could do other things for them.

As the morning azaan broke before light, it was our sign to leave. Ganesh said, Didi, please leave her here.

We were standing in a goonda's house. Could we say no? I looked at Putli. She had no expression on her face. I had to be quick. I turned to Hasina. I was not expecting anything from her. I took her aside and told her what Ganesh was asking. I said we could cook up an excuse about her periods or something. She heard me out, as if weighing her chances. She had seen the money flow. She was here to find a man.

It is all right; leave me here, she said.

Who was I to change her mind? I agreed after she assured me that she knew how to take care of herself. All those stories about her affairs with various men suddenly felt like they were of her own making and not majboori, helplessness.

Where do you live, didi? asked Ganesh. Do not worry, she will be back soon.

She returned later in the night with him. She was carrying several shopping bags. She had finally bagged a man. It showed in her confident gait. She was happy. I could smell trouble trailing her. That night, as I performed for Ganesh, he had eyes only for his new mistress. I was not jealous. I was never interested in goondas. I wanted to survive, not waste away.

Whose child is this? he asked, picking you up when he visited me.

Mine, I said.

He was a nice man. He called me didi to show he was not interested in me. But in doing so, it seemed to give him the permission to gain entry into my house as a brother. To romance my sister with her consent. To treat you fondly as an uncle. I did not mind it so much in the beginning, because he may have been a goonda outside, but he treated us with the utmost respect and kindness. I did not think of it as an act, maybe because I had not seen him behaving otherwise – so I did not know what else to do but receive him warmly in my house. Ganesh had a partner, Anjum. Hasina started flirting with him next, causing a rift between the two men.

I want you to be my wife, Anjum said to her.

No, she is mine, said Ganesh.

It was a typical scenario. Two men behaving badly over who owned her. They had a scuffle many a time when Hasina did not take a side. She angered me too. I was so enraged once that I slapped her for creating this ugly situation in my house.

You work so hard, you are a silly woman, she said to me. Look at me – I get what I want without even raising a finger.

She had it in her hazel-brown cat-like eyes. Bhurri aankhein toh thi hi uski, billiyon jaisi. Kanji aankhein. She could mesmerize whichever man looked at her.

Tell Ganesh to back off, said Anjum to me, flashing a pistol.

He thought Ganesh would listen to me as I was his mooh-boli behen, sworn sister, in the compound. I had seen guns and knew how to react in such situations. If we cowered, we would be bullied. Ganesh somehow became my guardian now. The boys in the compound started addressing me as didi. Hasina was busy flirting with every man she saw when Ganesh was away.

You talk to him directly, I said to Anjum. Do not involve me. He is your friend.

Anjum shot Ganesh in the thigh one day. One of their chamchas, sycophants, informed me about it, disrupting a mujra midway in Foras Road. Things had begun to take an ugly turn. If I sent Hasina away, they would still not leave me. If she stayed, someone would have to pay with their life.

One day, Anjum said to me, Are you not worried for your child? You send him to the crèche these days.

You were not in the room when he said that. My heart immediately started thudding. Where was my child? I panicked.

Usually, at this hour, you were out with Ashok on the Chowpatty. Suddenly, just the thought of you being away from me even for a moment began tearing my heart apart. What would I do in this world without my child?

You had started walking by now. Ashok had suggested putting you in a nearby crèche in the day to help you learn to play. The compound was not a good place for a child. There was no space in the room for you to play in the kotha. It seemed like a good idea to send you to a crèche. What Anjum was suggesting filled my heart with fear. What if he kidnapped you?

These goons knew how to manipulate the women in the kotha without even touching them. He was targeting you. His men followed my taxi to Foras Road, stood in dark corners to scare me; they tried all sorts of silent scare tactics to put pressure on me to send Hasina to Anjum. It worked for them. Bishu, a young goon

from Dilipda's gang, used to call me behen. He would often hang
around in the compound to distract Anjum's men.

The compound was infamous for gang wars at the time. One
time, Parkiya, a criminal, was released from jail. He came to the
compound drunk, and beat up Dilip's brother, Babu, for some
minor altercation. He slashed Babu's leg with a knife. Dilip was
furious. He told his boys to close the compound and turn the
lights off. His boys gheraoed Parkiya. Dilip stabbed him with
a sword.

I was watching all this from my room. Rajkumari asked me
to turn off the lights and move away from the window. We were
used to seeing these horrific crimes. Dilip's men were pimps in the
compound, overlooking the dhanda of some girls who went out,
providing security to the women.

Parkiya was from another gang, I think. I do not know why most
of these men clashed, but it was a frequent affair in the compound.
Over time, we became used to the violence, the music from our
rooms dimming the noise outside. Music and violence had found a
way to coexist peacefully.

Parkiya's mother came to identify her dead son's body lying
outside Akku aapa's door. She spat on her son's body and cursed
in Marathi, You should have killed a few before you died. It would
have made me famous.

Dilip was caught, but was released after a few months. The women
in the compound welcomed him with garlands and songs. He, too,
had a mistress in the compound.

Haji Mastan also used to come to Foras Road. He was a patron
of Nargis bai. He used to attend the mujras with his own set of
young women, who travelled with him at most times. I met him,
but never got a chance to perform for him. Some girls used to come
to see us too. They were usually call girls accompanying patrons to
hotel rooms later.

I have seen Dawood Ibrahim in the compound. He came a few times. But he never attended the mujras. Members of a rival gang had killed his brother, Shabbir. His mistress, Chitra, was picked up from the compound by Dawood's men for questioning, as it was rumoured that she had tipped off the rivals. Her life was spared.

With the violence growing, I contemplated leaving the city. Goons were the least of my worries about raising you in Bombay. I was more worried about either of us perishing in a fire.

Once, I was sleeping on the fourth floor in my friend Shireen's room after returning from Foras Road. My younger sister, Shanna, and Ashok were in my room on the first floor. The electric meters caught fire near the stairs on the ground floor. Shireen and I were sleeping without any hosh, consciousness. We were dead tired. We did not hear anything when the fire broke out in the morning. Shanna and Ashok ran out in the chaos. They must have thought that someone had informed us and we would be out too. A few girls, including me, were on the fourth floor.

Shireen woke up when the fire was reaching up and the screams were getting louder. From the window we could see Opera House, where the crowd had gathered.

Wake up, Shireen panicked. We are trapped in a fire.

My child! I cried out, even before I could gather my senses. I looked out of the window and saw Shanna yelling, Didi, didi, come down.

She was holding you in her arms. I smiled and told Shireen, My child is safe.

Farida, Shireen, a few other girls and I climbed up to the terrace. The firefighters arrived and guided us down through a narrow ladder they attached to the terrace.

Another time, there was a fire in Foras Road in one of the buildings where we were performing. It was not a big fire, but scary nonetheless. I was trapped on the first floor as the fire engulfed the staircase.

Khursheed was on the other side, crying that her child was trapped inside. I went to her room, wrapped her baby in my pallu and jumped over the wooden stairs. I fell down, but managed to protect the baby. I got bruises on my arms and legs, but they were immediately attended to with ointment and bandages. What if I had been seriously injured? How would I take care of you then? The fear of the unknown was affecting me.

The violence, the fire hazards, Hasina's tumultuous love life – all these things were adding up against your safety. How was I going to raise you in such an unstable environment? I packed up and was on a train back to Calcutta. I had left the room to Hasina, sent Ashok to my jijaji's house and escaped. With Ganesh in the hospital and Anjum trying to find Hasina, I let her take her own decisions. I did not want to sacrifice you or your safety for her. Hasina hid somewhere until Ganesh returned. Anjum and he fought again.

A year passed, I heard stories from Akku aapa that Hasina had found a new romantic interest in Foras Road. His name was Akbar, yet another goonda. Anjum was out of the picture by now. Ganesh had shifted to Delhi. These goondas claimed to belong to the disbanded gangs of Haji Mastan and Karim Lala. Akbar married Hasina. She left Congress House.

One more significant episode took place right after I left Congress House. Some filmmakers from London made a documentary on the courtesans of the kotha and Hasina was prominently featured in the story. She became keen to work in films because an international film crew had now discovered her. The documentary was shot in the compound.

Through Akbar, she began to meet filmmakers. She met Kirti. He was a sound recordist in B.R. Chopra Films. She soon left Akbar and began seeing Kirti. She used to think she looked like Reena Roy. She was plump like the heroine.

Hasina used to eat a lot. I remember how she salivated eyeing the beef kebabs outside Bacchu Seth Ki Wadi in Foras Road.

When I took her there, she spent most of her time eating and hanging out with the boys – and even bagged a butcher boyfriend at one point in time. No surprises there – she loved them with meat on their bones. I did not eat beef. I used to pack parcels for Akku aapa.

The kebabs were so popular that film stars used to come there in their big Impala cars. Rajesh Khanna's car was often spotted there. The crowd would yell with joy when his car entered the lane.

Hasina attended film parties to socialize with the stars. She got roles as an extra in the films of Anil Kapoor and Dharmendra. She thought it was just a matter of time before she made it. Kirti had stopped her from performing in dance clubs, where she used to go infrequently to perform in a dark room and earn a quick buck by flirting with drunken men. He told her it was not good for her image as a rising star.

Accha, yaad aaya, I remember, once I took Hasina with me on a film shoot where someone made us audition for a small role. I was rejected because of the scar mark on my forehead – my naseeb. Hasina got the part in *Jhutha Sach*. She was shown gliding down an escalator to be photographed by child actor Jugal Hansraj.

The rising star Hasina was on a descent after her beginner's luck!

Kirti kept her in a flat in Andheri East, but she was on a tight leash. She could not step out without his permission. She felt stifled in her ambition to be a star and found herself not making any progress beyond side parts in television pilots and films.

She left Kirti for a gutka baron. Now, I have completely forgotten his name, but I think he had something to do with a popular gutka brand. He was a lumpy old man, carrying bags of money in his car. He was smitten by her film-star aspirations and wanted to fund her career. He lavished her with gold ornaments and expensive clothes. She amassed a lot of jewellery in this period. He used to live in Ahmedabad and would travel to meet her in Bombay or Poona.

Hasina's family started milling around her. Her brother, his wife, their children – they all began to treat her as the breadwinner of the house as they took on more passive roles as her sycophants.

She enjoyed this sudden sense of power she had in the Kanjarbhat community, where the men thought of her as a shiny foreign object trying to re-enter the samaaj, society. She had spent many years living away, not entirely out of choice, but as a commodity that was sold in another flashier market. She wanted to be accepted back within the community and even find a suitable man to settle down with. The gutka baron was only a weekend distraction. She could steer two boats on the choppy waters of her life, or so she thought.

Hasina started to perform more often in dance bars. The Kanjarbhat sarpanch, Morchand, in our small community in Pimpri was enamoured by her. She decided to live in a slum. She was looking after her family too.

I met her on one of my visits to the city and advised her to move out of the hut and return to a clean environment. She did not listen to me.

After a few years, the gutka baron began to bore her. It was rumoured that she pushed him off a bridge somewhere in Poona, with help from Morchand. They wanted to take his money and get rid of him. Luckily, he survived the fall with only a few fractures. He never returned to Poona after that. He died a few years later. She went to his family to ask for her share of money. They chased her out.

When the money was over and the jewellery had disappeared, she began selling desi daaru, local alcohol, in her hut. She started seeing lots of local men at the time – rickshaw drivers, shopkeepers, truck drivers and all sorts of useless drunkards, drug peddlers and gamblers. Morchand began avoiding her. She was ageing and had become bitter, drinking more than earning from it. She also kept losing the money she made by investing it in satta, gambling. Her family abandoned her.

I was visiting my younger sister Rohini when I heard that Hasina was seriously ill. She had dengue. She was admitted to Nirma Hospital in Pimpri. I remember it so clearly. It was a few days after Navaratri. I had returned from the temple of Tuljadevi near Solapur. I was in Waki when I heard the news and rushed to Pimpri. I saw her in an almost unconscious state, unable to speak or even move her eyelids. All she did was shed tears – it never ceased to flow, as if a dam of feelings behind her eyes had finally broken. She wept for three whole days.

On the fourth day, I saw the staff taking her body to the morgue. I stopped them, checked if it was her and informed everyone. The doctors had not notified us. They put her in the morgue and asked us to clear her dues. I was low on cash, so I pawned my gold chain to contribute some money to the fund. Her family searched her hut for money, but all they found was a worthless metal bangle. The box of jewellery she once owned was empty.

The hospital staff refused to hand over her body for cremation. The Kanjar samaj raised about fifty thousand rupees in cash to retrieve her body. When we were clearing her dues, we found out that she had been admitted in the name of Reena. Reema who became Hasina who became 'Reena Roy'. She never got a chance to be a star in life, but in death, she was trying to arrive in heaven in style.

Calcutta

Khair, back then, when Hasina caused so much trouble in my life, I returned to Calcutta for your safety. Everything returned to normal in some time. Sarita, to whom I had sublet my room, had kept things in order. She gave it back to me and moved to another room. Nothing felt out of place, although it took a few weeks for patrons to return to my room.

I had to start all over again, but this time restarting was not difficult because I had mastered the art of the return. My return worked to my advantage, having performed in Bombay for film stars and gangsters. A Bombay bai was considered more glamorous. My new wardrobe, featuring the latest trends and designs from Hindi-film heroines, added to the sheen. Your father's friends came to see me. I warned them to not bring him there.

If you bring him here, I will break his legs, I said.

I think the Bombay lifestyle had made my tongue sharper. But how was he going to stay away for long? Khan saab came after a few months. By then, I had calmed down and knew I was going to treat him like the other patrons. I had no place for him in my heart.

Sometimes, when a drunken brawl took place in the kotha, we would be summoned to the local police station. I befriended some officers; in fact, Meena and I even danced in the station to disco songs like '*Aap jaise koi*' and '*Laila main laila*'. We had to amp it up a little, slightly on the chaalu, cheap side, if I may say so myself, because we were inside a police station, where it was mostly done for fun. It was surreal to be performing there, but it was always safe. The officers did not treat us like prostitutes. They were aware of our connections with local goons. At the Lal Bazaar thana, we entertained officers from the detective department. These were men to be on good terms with so that the goons also understood that we had the power and support of the law. When the officers had a festive programme, they called us to perform, or when they came to the kotha they were treated as VIP guests and that made them feel important – as respected upholders of women's rights. We were cunning in our dealings with the law. We totally pandered to them for our own gains.

In my free time, I spent my energies in looking for a school for you. I wanted to keep you away from this world. It was not the kind of place to raise a boy. A girl was not raised but groomed here. What did I know of how to raise a boy here? What would I groom you here for? A goonda, a dalla, an ustad? I was not going to turn you into a wreck.

A teacher used to visit me. I told him to help me. His name was Giriji. He said he was going to put his son in a boarding school in Kurseong. He said it would be the best place for you. I gave him some money to fetch the admission form.

You have to come with me to Kurseong, he said.

I went along with him by train. He, his son, you and I. We checked into our separate hotel rooms and met the principal,

Bhanu Pratap, of Little Flower School. The principal enrolled you without asking any questions. You were admitted into lower kindergarten. He asked me for your father's name while writing your details. I said my jijaji, Anoop Gagade's, name because I could not say Khan saab's name. I panicked, thinking a Hindu woman using a Muslim man's name would lead to trouble with your admission. I was not even married to Khan saab. How could I say his name? Anoop Gagade was Babbo's husband. He would not have a problem if he found out that I had used his name to get you admitted in school. Who would tell him, anyway? He was far, far away. I myself would tell him later, and he would understand. Anyway, when I uttered his name hesitantly, the principal could not understand my words. So I repeated, Anoop Gagade. When he asked one more time, I got nervous. Can you spell it out? he asked. I got cold feet.

Aap likh dijiye, you write it, I said.

He thought for a moment, put his pen to paper and asked, Is it Anoop Gaekwad?

Haan, yes, I said. Wahi hai. Jo aapne kaha. Exactly as you said. Anoop Gae ... Gae ... Gaekwad! I smiled nervously. Bas, from then your name was officially written as Manish Gaekwad.

Dekhiye, look, I said to the principal, my son is a delicate boy; he is a quiet, well-behaved child. Please give him special care and keep him away from noisy children. I began sobbing as I said so. I was worried about leaving you so far away in a school, but was also trying to convince myself that this was the best thing for my little boy.

Do not worry, he said, we will look after him with special care.

Bhanu Pratap patted me and tried to cheer me up. I believed him. I had no choice. I was doing it for your safety. You cried, not understanding what was happening. You were used to seeing me say tata and bye-bye as I used to go out to perform, but since you did not have any concept of time then, you did not know how long it would take for me to return. You waved back at me, as if you would see me the next morning.

After six months or so, Bhanu Pratap sent a letter saying you were now promoted to upper kindergarten. I was happy that you were making such quick progress in your studies.

The next year, when I was playing Holi, a letter arrived. It said, Your son is in the hospital. Please come soon.

I boarded the next train. They had operated on your chin to remove a gilti, swelling. You were kept in the Himalay Hospital for a few days. I stayed beside you, but I could not bear to sit by your side when the nurses came to dress your wound. I could not bear to see even a scratch on you. I used to walk out, and pray to god and sob.

Mummy, I am fine, you said.

I think those were your first words to me. You were such a quiet child that anything you might have said before had not registered with me. You were a late speaker. And now you were speaking, and speaking fluently, like an angrezi baccha!

I was not expecting you to speak when your face was bandaged up in the hospital.

Mummy, I am fine, you repeated.

It made my heart weep.

You spoke such clean, fluent English. I cried even more. My child was going to have a better future than me. That was all I could think of when you used those English words.

Mummy, I am fine.

In that moment, I knew you were going to be fine going forward. Finer than I ever had a chance to be. You wrote letters to me – I could not read or understand your words, but your crooked handwriting was enough to glue my breaking heart together. The masterji would read your letters to me. You used to write, Please come to meet me; I love you very much. Please send me a bottle of pickle. We bonded over our love for pickles.

You came home for your winter vacation.

Mummy, where is my fork and spoon? you asked, when I served you dinner on the floor where we sat and ate. I called the other tawaifs and said, Dekh, kitni phatt-phatt angrezi bolta hai yeh toh. See how fluently he speaks in English.

I wiped my happy tears and asked you to repeat the question.

Phir se bol, I said. Yeh fork kya hai? Say it again. What is this fork?

I knew of forks as kaantas, but I had never heard what it was called in English before. I did not own a fork in my kitchen because I never ate any food that required it. I had seen it in restaurants, but we ate with our hands at home. So I had to go to the market to buy forks when you explained to me that the fork was missing in the plate next to the spoon. My son, you were an education to me. You were my education.

You used to open your books and read nursery rhymes. I used to stare and wonder what you were reading. It was music to my ears. Better than our music. It sounded bright and positive, full of rhythm and dance in your rising cadence. It was unlike the lives my siblings and I had ever lived.

This new foreign language that you spoke was the language of the rich and the prosperous. It did not belong in a kotha. That alone reassured me that you were going to do better things in life. You were going to be better than me. That is what I wanted for you. I had wanted it for my sister Shanna and my brother Dasrath too, but they were not interested in studying. You were sent to boarding school even before you could think. You learnt etiquette and good manners, and your first language was English. You would not talk to someone who spoke in Hindi, because that was the rule in school. So unless someone spoke to you in your language, you kept your own quiet company.

You were different because I made sure you got to education before it reached you. My siblings saw poverty before I tried to educate them. They were used to living without hope. They saw no future in education. They were used to living in a certain, undisciplined and, if I can say so, dirty and filthy environment. For them, education was an obstacle, a hurdle that I had put in their path. I was asking them to jump over it. They preferred to crawl under it. My efforts with them failed.

It was because of them, I should say, that I owed it to you. My failure with them gave me greater clarity that you should not miss even a day of school from the very beginning. The boarding school was the perfect solution – it was like a vault and I was keeping you in a safe-deposit box. It was just like a bank. It would pay dividends on maturity of full term.

Luckily for me, the principal in Kurseong did not ask me much about your father. He assumed I was a housewife. Whenever he came to Calcutta, he would meet Giriji. I met him too, but never mentioned my work or my house. Giriji was also a discreet man, so he kept my secret from the principal. We met as friends, but maintained a cordial distance. A few years later, it was time to transfer you to another school.

We only have classes up to Class Two in this school, the principal told me. You will have to find another school for your son now.

Why don't you find one for him? I asked.

I also asked you if you wanted to study in Kurseong or Darjeeling, where the big schools were.

Darjeeling, you said. You even knew the spelling of that long word. You spelt it out for me when I asked if you knew where it was. Up a hill – you showed me the mountains. The school had taken you there for a toy-train ride once, you said.

The principal sent me to an all-boys school in Darjeeling. I think it was St. Paul's School or North Point. I met the principal there. He was dressed like a father in a church. He immediately admitted you.

I was shown around the school. It was huge. I saw some boys playing in the grounds. I thought, How will my quiet, delicate boy fit in with them? They looked like giants compared to you. You were so tiny, shy and frail. I began to worry. I decided not to put you with the big boys.

I went to another school: West Point. It was on top of a hill. The climb was steep and arduous. I liked how small it was. There was a mix of small and big kids in the playground. Both boys and girls, just like in Little Flower. I felt comfortable in this environment. The principal said that the local kids also studied in the school, not just outstation rich kids. That made me feel better. The school was small and it felt like the education was very hands-on. The principal asked for your name and did not make you sit for a test. Everything felt right. Except when he asked me about your father. I said he was dead. I used my jijaji's name. He did not ask me any more.

I took you aside and told you that if anyone asked about your father, you were to say he was dead.

You nodded. You were such a smart boy. You understood things without questioning them. I left you there and walked downhill. You were a good student with good grades. When you came to the kotha for your winter vacation, I realized that you should have a separate home as you grew up. Where would your friends come? Not to the kotha!

That thought started bothering me. One day, I asked Khan saab to help me find a flat. We were on cordial terms by then. In the kotha, we may want to get rid of a man, but we cannot stop them from visiting us. I had moved on after him, but he had not. I was indifferent to him, not insolent. His friends would attend my mujras. He was in their company. I could not be entirely dismissive of him. When I had returned to Calcutta, I knew that, at some point, we would meet. I could not avoid him.

Khan saab thought that helping me would gain him entry into my heart. It did and it did not. He showed me an under-construction property near New Market. I was short of thirty thousand rupees to hand over as advance for the property. I asked him if he could lend me the money.

I do not have so much money, he said. I can help you as long as you do not need to borrow from me.

He had once taken a diamond nose pin from me and set it into a ring in his finger. It was worth more than the money I needed to pay. I had bought the nose pin from a Marwari businessman, who had to sell it to fund his wife's surgery. He had sold it to me for fifteen thousand rupees, as that was the exact amount he needed. He said it was worth more. It must have been. I had not checked its worth. Khan saab had. He removed it from my nose and pocketed it, saying he would bring it back set as a ring. Sometimes, in a moment of passion, one cannot always sense a lie. It gets cloudy. I could have asked him to return the diamond to me. It was shining on his finger when I performed in the mujra. It was staring at me. But could I shame him for stealing it from me? He was a loud man; he would make a big fuss about me having gifted it to him. I was helpless.

It was then that I decided to go to Bombay and check my bank account. There was a bank near Opera House, where an agent, Arun bhai, used to collect and submit money in an account. I did not know much about it then, but some girls used to trust him with their bank work, so I followed their advice. I even invested in some fixed deposit or life insurance – I cannot recollect exactly now.

I met Arun bhai and said, I need my money. How much have I deposited?

Twenty-five thousand, he said.

He deducted his commission and paid me the remaining amount. I did not get any clarity on the fixed deposit or life insurance, whatever it was; I had money that was stuck in that as well. He said it would mature later. I did not understand it, so I let it go, saying that I would check on it later. It must have been another twenty-five thousand.

I left for Poona after that. I met my mother and said, Lend me some money.

I do not have any, Gullo said. As usual.

Somehow, I managed to get another ten thousand from her. I had given her a lot of money all these years. She had been storing it in pots and pans all over the house. It had to be unearthed now. She used to stitch the money into a mattress. I returned to Calcutta. I went to the developer and paid the advance. I got the house about two years later. I took you along on the day they called me to claim the owner's bill for the flat.

In whose name should we issue the bill? asked the developer.

My name and my son's name, I said.

What is your name? he asked.

Rekha, I said.

The developer was taken aback. He had assumed that I was a Muslim lady, because I was introduced to him by Khan saab. Khan saab must have told them I am his wife or something. Everyone was told my name was Rehana, except me. I found out only much later. Since I had paid for the house, naturally, I wanted it in my name. The developer had assumed it would be in Khan saab's name or my so-called Muslim name, Rehana, by which he used to address and introduce me to people outside.

Oh, aap Hindu hain? he said.

Ji, I said. So is my child. The bill should name us both.

So Khan saab is not your husband? he asked.

I thought they would create a problem if I denied it. The flat was in a Muslim ghetto. The developer was Muslim. Maybe they preferred Muslims.

Woh apni jagah hain, main apni jagah hoon, I said. He is at his place, I am at mine.

The developer understood that I was trying to be discreet.

He gave me the bill.

How could you go alone and get the house registered in your name? Khan saab asked. He fought with me when he found out from them.

You have insulted me, he said. My prestige, my reputation is ruined.

What to do? I said. I am the one who paid for the house. It belongs to me. How is your prestige, your reputation ruined? Get lost.

He would not get lost so easily. I did not have money for the furniture. I again asked him if he could give me some money for the furniture, at least.

Oh, you are incorrigible, he said. I am talking about my reputation and you want money from me all the time. I do not have any money; go burn yourself.

While the furniture was being made, he managed to get another set of keys made for the main door.

I will see to it that the carpenters work hard, he said.

I came by only on the weekends. Beds, tables, chairs, sofas, cabinets, almirahs – all sort of woodwork was in progress.

Only a few tenants had moved in. I was not planning to move in, and thought of using it as a holiday home when you returned from the boarding school for your winter vacation.

I had no clue that Khan saab was using the house to bring his friends over for midnight parties. Girls from Sonagachi were coming to the house. There was food, sex and drinks in the house as if it were a den for pleasure.

It so happened that, once, you were with me in the house. We had returned from Bandook Gully after my mujra. You were not sleepy, so we were sitting and talking.

Suddenly, a car stopped outside. You saw it from the balcony that it was your father. You knew he was your father, but you were also told not to acknowledge him as your father in school. I do not know how you processed this information, but you did not ask questions and only followed my instructions.

Papa, you said, when you saw him on the street.

You waved to him. He climbed up the stairs.

Go, open the door, I told you.

You ran to the door and, when you saw him, said, Is this any time to come home?

He walked in and asked, What are you doing here?

What do you mean, I said. This is my house.

No sooner had I said this than I heard a car below the balcony. I looked down and saw a few of Khan saab's friends there, like Eshwar and Pawan. Two girls were talking loudly. I understood what this was all about. I snatched the house keys from him. Khan saab tried to grab it back. We got into a scuffle. You ran and hugged me, crying and shouting, Leave my mummy!

Khan saab was asking me to leave. I was asking him to leave. I ran to the kitchen. I poured a can of mitti ka tel, kerosene oil, on myself. I was holding a box of matchsticks.

If you do not leave now, I said, I will set myself on fire.

I was screaming in rage.

Get out of my house, I was shouting.

Some oil had spilt on him as well.

My neighbours, a Muslim family, ran into my house, trying to stop us. Khan saab's friends ran away with the girls. I threw a quilt over you as you sat on the bed, and watched in horror from under it.

When the neighbours took me to the other room to pacify me, Khan saab pulled you out from the quilt and left.

I did not know what to do next. I did not know where he lived. I did not have a phone in the house. I could only wait for him in the kotha in Bandook Gully the next day. I could not go to the police to report the kidnapping of my child. I knew he would come to his senses and return you. He had snatched you away from me at the railway station once before. This was expected of him.

I had not expected what he did next. He sent a message through his friend to meet me at Victoria Garden. He said I could have my child back for thirty thousand rupees.

I went with the money. I remember it was a cold December afternoon, nothing as cold as that moment when I had to secure your freedom from your own greedy father who was torturing us. This man had held his own child for ransom. How much lower could he fall?

We sat on a bench. I gave him the money. I took you in my arms and wept.

I am warning you, I said. I will go to the police if I ever see you anywhere close to the kotha or my house again.

After that day, he disappeared from our lives. But not for too long.

Khan saab may have sired many children, but did not care for anyone. Once, a young girl named Razia came to Bandook Gully from Sitarampur. She claimed to be Khan saab's daughter. She waited for him in the kotha. He did not arrive. Word used to travel fast about such things. If he were sitting in another kotha, he would have heard of Razia's sudden appearance and avoided visiting Bandook Gully. She left as mysteriously as she had arrived. I do not know what happened of her, but her existence was a sign of the neglect you could face. I could not completely remove Khan saab from our lives. I did want you to see your father. I knew some day you would ask, Where is my father? I want to see him. I had to compromise on my principles.

Around this time, Putput had begun to harass us in the kotha. Putput's daadi, grandmother, had owned the kotha. She had donated the kotha to the Waqf Board when she died. Her family was living on the premises. Putput's sister, Hasina, was also a tawaif. Putput had grown up with two brothers, Pona and Mahfooz. All of them were good-for-nothings. They were allegedly involved in illegal businesses, like satta and gundagardi, gambling and hooliganism.

They forced Hasina to stop singing and dancing. Putput became the mutwalli, manager of the kotha. He wanted to put a stop to our business because he wanted to turn a new leaf as a respectable crook.

The kotha also had an imambara where the Shia family used to assemble during the month of Ramzan for majlis, an assembly for worship. Putput began to organize the majlis with fanfare and then used the occasion to not issue our rent bills. He sent us an eviction notice through court. He had filed a case against us.

Some of us owned the rooms under a salaami system, where we paid a lumpsum on acquisition and a nominal monthly rental. I had paid twelve thousand rupees for the room. The rent was rupees two hundred and fifty. Since the kotha was under the Waqf Board, it could not be sold and we could not be asked to leave. On what grounds was he asking us to leave? He was saying that the premise was for religious purposes, where it was illegal to perform mujras.

We had a licence to perform as artistes. An agent made a certificate for us, which we framed and hung in our rooms for police verification. The agent went to the corporation to make it. We were recognized entertainers.

Putput would not issue us our rent bills to make it look like we were not paying rent and living illegally. This went on for a year. Some bais panicked and started paying him a fat amount to appease

him. Kamandal aapa and I decided to go to the rent control office
in Dalhousie.

We spoke to some officials and told them that the mutwalli was
not issuing our rent bills. They asked us to pay in the office instead.
We did as we were told. Now Putput would have to get our rent
money from the office. He would have to pay a penalty to collect it
from there. This was how we fought him for many years.

Then Putput started heckling the patrons. Putput and his boys
would break the street lamps leading to Bandook Gully. Any patron
who ventured further was frisked and interrogated. Some were
chased away. Frequent quarrels and fights erupted in the street.

The bais started moving out one by one. First, the ground floor
emptied out. Meena, who used to live beside me on the first floor,
was the first to go. Mallika aapa had long gone. Geeta left. Meera,
Baby, Sunita, all of them who had sublet the houses, left.

Suman was a beautiful woman on the ground floor. She spoke
less, sang ghazals in a low timbre. The owner of Hind Cinema fell
in love with her. She quickly became his mistress and gave up the
profession, moving out of Bandook Gully.

Jhumki was another famous tawaif. She was a young girl who
infused the sagging profession with vitality. She was a superb dancer.
A queue would form as patrons struggled to get to her room. Despite
her popularity, she was not able to hold out longer because her room
was right below Hasina's, Putput's sister. He was not going to let her
shine and her fame spread.

Around this time, another dreaded goonda was making our lives
worse. Omar was a laheem-shaheem, healthy and fit, handsome
young man, who was a notorious criminal involved in satta and
extortion. He was called the Bengal Tiger. When Indira Gandhi
visited the city, he is rumoured to have escorted her out of the airport.
He had close ties with politicians in the Congress party. We just

knew that he was the secretary of the Mohammedan Sporting Club. The office was in Chuna Gully. Once, I was at home, eating dinner around 11 p.m., when his dalal came to see me.

Rekha, he said, Omar saab wants to meet you.

I panicked. Why did he want to see me? When his pimp came, it meant only one thing – the girl had been summoned for sex.

While the realization was just sinking in, he added, In Sattawandi.

I was relieved. Sattawandi was another kotha nearby. I often went there to perform if parties sent word.

Kiske kamre mein? I asked. In whose room?

Chidiya bai ke yahan, he said. In Chidiya bai's room.

Accha, I said, trying to gulp down the food sitting like a piece of rock in my mouth. My appetite dropped.

Okay, I said, let me change.

I followed him.

When he saw me approaching, Omar said, Pahadan. He used to call me a mountain girl. He was not attracted to the rustic kind. His women had to be sophisticated, delicate and shy. I was the opposite.

Arre, aa na, come, pahadan, he said. Suna hai tu Bambai se naya dance seekh ke aayi hai. I heard you have learnt some new Bombay dance.

I noticed that some men I had entertained in Bombay were sitting with him. They were his guests.

Rekha, tu, you? one of them said.

I felt like cursing him, but smiled instead.

I danced to a few songs for them. A mix of dance and romantic numbers like '*Mujhe naulakha manga de re*' and '*Jab hum jawaan honge*'.

Omar was slightly eccentric. While I danced, he cut the hair of one of his men. It was disconcerting to watch and perform at the same time. He was known to pull out his revolver and shoot at the ceiling if he liked the performance. I was trying to not reach that level of perfection, because making him happy could be a disaster for me if he decided to pick me up for his guests.

The miraasis who played the musical instruments were also frightened and played wonkily.

After the so-so performance, Omar said, Baith, main aa raha hoon. Sit, I'll be back.

I felt gutted. I thought he was stepping out to make arrangements as to which of his useless friends could have me for the night. The good thing was that these men had not yet paid me for the performance, so I began thinking that they did not like it and decided to leave. Omar was not impressed by my Bombay dance.

I waited for an hour, then another. The birds had begun to wake up. It was time for me to be in my own nest, snuggling with my child, who was home on vacation. What was I waiting for?

Chidiya, I am not feeling well. Can I go? I asked the hostess.

Let him come, she said, then you leave with your money.

Who cares, money can come later, I said. My health is important right now. What is money without us?

Chidiya sympathized.

I do not think he will come back, I said. And his chamchas who are still hanging around here will leave on their own.

She mustered up the courage to tell one of Omar's men that I was not feeling well. She added her bit to make it sound worse.

I left just as it was beginning to get bright. The streets were empty. The dogs were sleeping. There was an eerie silence all around. The only sound cutting through the still air was the payal on my ankles as I tried to tiptoe home.

Omar had probably returned to his office and forgotten all about me. He had never shown any interest in me previously, and despite the men who requested for my midnight Bombay dance, he did not find it captivating. Maybe that also explained why he was so disinterested and was giving a haircut to one of his men. No woman could have said no to Omar, but not saying no is different from giving our permission.

I have been pursued by many goondas, but I never gave in. A goonda named Irshad once came with a revolver to threaten me. He had had his eyes on me ever since he saw me perform in Ramkali ki baari. He followed me from kotha to kotha in the hope that I would cosy up with him.

Tere ko to main dekh loonga – chhodunga nahi. I will not leave you, he used to say when I used to dismiss his advances.

Tu chhod chahe nahi chhod, tere haath mein nahi aane waali, I said. Whether you leave me or not, I will not go with you.

I knew that if I appeared weak, he would control me. He would usually try to corner me alone. But that worked in my favour. I could also fight back, knowing that there was no one else around to intimidate me. Yeh lo, woh Bandook Gully mein bandook taan raha tha, par main hati nahi. He was pulling out a gun in Bandook Gully, but I stood my ground. Irshad was an unattractive rogue who had little success in snaring a mistress. He could not get Rani, so now he was after me. In Bandook Gully, he used to come for Meena's mujra. Whenever I saw him, I would slip into my room and draw the curtains shut, remove my make-up and evening clothes to look as ordinary and unappealing as possible. He tried to barge into my room. I pushed back.

Chala goli, shoot, I said. Tere mein himmat hai, toh chala. If you have the guts, shoot me. I once cried out dramatically in front of everyone as witness, facing him and dropping my pallu. All the other girls were watching. He would never be able to get away with it had he pulled the trigger.

It just so happened that Khan saab arrived that day and saw the pistol drawn. Khan saab knew some small-time crooks as well.

Abbe jaa, get lost, he said to Irshad. Do you not know she is my wife?

After that day, Irshad never showed his face to me again.

I should have thanked Khan saab, but I did not need to. After Irshad left, I told Khan saab that he was not going to get anything for it. I knew how to handle rogues. He was just better dressed!

There was another goon, Rab, who was growing in popularity around this time. He used to hang around the stairs of the kotha, checking out the girls, trying to get friendly with them. He grew into a monster later, calling girls to his terrace adda above the Bow Bazaar post office. But he paid the girls. He did not want them to sing or dance for him. All he wanted was sex.

Another time, when my cousin sister, Rajjo, was with me, he came with Omar to Moni didi's room downstairs and asked for me.

As usual, Omar called out, seeing me descend the stairs, O, pahadan, suna tere yahan koi ladki aayi hai. I heard you have a new girl.

Haan, yes, I said.

I rushed back upstairs, and instructed Rajjo to look as simple and unattractive as possible. She removed her make-up and wore a dull salwar-kurta. I thought it would do the trick.

Oh! Omar exclaimed when he saw her and said nothing.

He was looking for a beautiful girl like Kavita, like Suman – girls he had taken in the past. Rajjo was young, about sixteen or seventeen, not very pretty and new to the kotha. She did not know the customs of the trade yet.

Salaam kar. Greet them, I said.

She did as asked, and kept her head down. I knew that Omar had rejected her immediately. But for Rab, a new girl was fresh meat. He was not particular about beauty.

That night, around midnight, he sent his pimp for Rajjo. I could not stop her. I was helpless because, if I refused, your life could be in danger – forget hers and mine. You were a child still. I explained to Rajjo what this meant. We wondered if it was worth telling the pimp that Rajjo had got scared and run away. The crooks would not buy it so easily, though. They would still harass me. I had seen what Rab had done to Tillo, another bai.

Rajjo understood that if she wanted to stay in the kotha with me, she would have to pay a price first. We cried, but our tears dried quickly, before these men turned them to blood.

Rajjo had come to me like Hasina had in Bombay. Even Laxmi, another cousin sister, had come to me. I have seen all of these cousin sisters come to me and ruin themselves eventually. I think I managed to stay alive for a long time because I was groomed from a very young age. I saw a lot of bais losing it before I became one myself. These cousin sisters did not get taleem, training, from a young age – they came when they either ran away from home, were ostracized for their burre lacchan, bad reputation, or when the glamour of the craft attracted them. I was here to survive. I was not going to let anything come in between me and my will to live. Khair, that is me.

Dekh, look, Rajjo, do as he says, I said, and no one will be hurt.

She knew she would be damaged for the rest of her life, but she was willing to go. She wanted to be a tawaif. She had chosen to come here out of her own free will.

That was one of the longest nights of my life. I did not sleep. I stayed awake, worried for her safety and return. She had gone without hesitation and returned in the morning with cash. It was the price she paid and earned back for her career in the kotha. When she came back, her eyes remained lowered. We did not speak of what had happened. We just hugged each other and wept.

It made us stronger in embrace. Two women holding each other to move on and make the best of what we have. We had only each other to look out for, our bonds strengthened in the kotha in a way that I cannot fully comprehend or explain. It was a sisterhood that empowered us, instead of making us feel helpless and weak. And we moved on with alarming speed because we had to survive it, not allow it to destroy us.

Unfortunately, Rajjo did not last long in the kotha. She was no good at singing and dancing, despite her best efforts. Maybe the trauma of that incident had started eating her from the inside. Since she did not excel in mujras, she fell in love with the first guy who proposed. She grew comfortable with night-outs in hotel rooms with various men. She found it easier to do the other thing that we – the older, trained tawaifs – resisted. Or what was the difference between sex workers and us? We were trying to live with a little dignity – or at least asking for that dignity, working for it. Sex work in Sonagachi was an altogether different profession. If we wanted to do it, why were we putting up such a show every night?

Sab ki apni apni majboori hoti hai. Everyone has their constraints.

I do not condemn sex work, but I worked hard to live my life with a little respect and dignity, which came with being a tawaif. It gave me motivation to live with my head held high. Perhaps the other kind of work would not have given me the same feeling. I had seen the girls in Sonagachi living in worse conditions than us. I did not want to be a slave to some pimp, some madame, or even the patrons who could dictate to us. I had agency as a tawaif. I had my own room, I had a choice to perform in the kotha, in hotel rooms, on stage functions. I had a loyal audience, adulation and, most importantly, money to improve the lives of my siblings for the better. I even had a choice in the man I wanted to be seen with. Poori azaadi. Full freedom.

Along with Rajjo, Laxmi actually arrived with a baby in her tummy – so she did not have to go through the initiation by goons. She, too, was not good at the job. They both left after two or three years. I never once tried to use them to make money.

And Rab, he was a laundiyabaaz – skirt chaser. He fell in love with Tillo. Her real name was Sunita. She was very pretty and fair. She could sing and dance. When she moved to Bandook Gully, he immediately trapped her. Initially, we were friends with her, but after she began seeing Rab, we distanced ourselves. He married her and took her to his house. Then her real troubles began, because the man was not going to stop sleeping with other girls just because he had got a wife. She threw a fit. They quarrelled often. When she was three months pregnant, he took her to his village somewhere in Uttar Pradesh.

Some allege that he pushed her off the terrace. When she did not die, he choked and killed her. It was brutal. All the girls in the kotha were horrified. There was a case filed against him, the police were on the lookout. He went underground and never returned to Bandook Gully. Tillo had a son from a previous lover. He lives in Delhi. He is gay. Hormone ki gadbadi ho gayi, maine suna; theek se ilaaj hota to theek ho jaata. I heard he has hormone issues; he could have been cured if he was treated on time.

Phullo's brother, Suresh, was also a gunda. When I came to live in Bandook Gully, he used to live downstairs with his sisters Moni didi and Sakuntala didi.

He was a young boy in his early twenties. He used to be a dada in the mohalla. He used to collect chanda for festivities. He never argued with me about anything. Suresh then started hanging out with Rashid Khan, another small-time crook, who would later be arrested for the Bow Bazaar bomb blast in 1993. They started an illegal satta-matka, gambling, business. Their rise was immediate.

They made lots of money. Rashid started using the money to buy several properties – restaurants, flats and other businesses. Putput and Pona, these two brothers, were also part of it, but broke away from the gang afterwards. Suresh bought a flat and moved out of Bandook Gully. He was in love with Kiran, of the Sapna–Kiran sisters who used to live in Bandook Gully. He took them along with him.

Now, Omar had his own gang of thugs in the same area. Naturally, they were going to clash. Omar asked Suresh for fifty thousand rupees. Suresh refused to give him the money. Omar charmed his sister, Phullo. Phullo loved playing the peacemaker, but usually added more fuel first. Phullo sided with Omar.

On a Diwali night, Omar told Phullo, See, tell your brother I need the money urgently.

Suresh saw him and abused him. Omar could not tolerate being humiliated by the boy in a kotha. He could not do anything there. He left with a plan.

Omar went to Sattawandi to cool off in Chidiya bai's room. He probably needed the money to shower on girls. It was festival night – he had to show off. Suresh, not knowing he was there, also landed up in the kotha, but in another tawaif's room. They were both in the middle of a mujra performance when Omar was informed about Suresh's presence in the kotha.

Bano aapa, Rashid's cousin sister, used to live in Sardar ki baari. She heard that Omar and Suresh were both in the same kotha. She did not let Rashid step out of the house that night. She kept the Quran on the doorstep.

You will have to step over the Quran paak if you go out, Bano told him.

Bano was feared by the tawaifs. She was Putli bai's daughter – a tawaif who had joined daku Maan Singh's gang of baaghis, rebels, in Agra. Daku Sultana had asked her to surrender after the police killed Maan Singh. Putli bai lost an arm in a fight. I do not know how she died. She had sent Bano with her elder sister to Calcutta. Bano also worked as a tawaif. She retired when her children grew up. Later, Bano married a pimp, Qasim. Qasim and Salim were two notorious pimps, who later branched into satta and raised an empire of shady businesses, in which Rashid was now actively involved.

Rashid was trapped in his own house as Bano did not allow him to leave home. Phullo got the news about Suresh and Omar being in the same kotha, but did nothing. Omar called Sajid, one of his henchmen, to pick Suresh up from the kotha. Suresh ran in the nick of time and hid in Qausar's room. He slipped under the bed. Somehow, he was found. They dragged him out. They took him to their club in Chuna Gully.

Please spare me, he said. I will leave with my family right now.

Omar was in no mood for an apology. He came off as a sensible man, but when he was insulted, he could not be mollified.

His men beat Suresh and stabbed him multiple times. Omar then tonsured his head. He was always messing with people's hair. Omar left the club, telling his men to fix Suresh.

Sajid, whom Suresh had once thrashed on the streets, was not going to show any mercy. He chopped off Suresh's penis and his naked body was dumped outside Islamia Hospital.[2]

We got news of this incident in the morning. We rushed to the hospital at once. He was still breathing. He died after seeing us. The post-mortem said he had forty-five injuries on his body. A group of tawaifs filled the hospital with their cries. One of their loved ones had been brutally hacked to death.

Omar was arrested from Free School Street. He was shitting when he was pulled out of the toilet. Kallu, Kamandal aapa's son, had become a gunda as well and was a friend of Suresh's. He abused

2   https://indiankanoon.org/doc/575647/

Omar in the police station. Omar barked back, saying he was going to deal with him when he got out.

After fifteen–sixteen years of trial, the seven accused were sentenced to ten years of imprisonment, but, by then, the kothas were out of business and many had been razed to the ground.

Years later, Kallu died in the 1993 bomb blast that wrecked the kotha district of Bow Bazaar. I think it was in the month of Ramzan. It was the night of 16 March when we heard a very loud sound in Bandook Gully. We immediately understood that there had been a blast somewhere close by. Bano aapa came to Bandook Gully that night because her house in Sardar ki baari had been damaged. We served her tea and discussed arrangements for her to scatter her family across the city. We knew the blast had something to do with Rashid, but who was going to ask and confirm at this hour?

The next day, the bais in the kotha – Meena, Phullo, Baby, Meera and I – went to the tramline and saw the site. The police had cordoned it off. People were clearing the rubble. Severed hands, feet, torsos and heads were popping out of the ruins. A huge crowd had gathered. The media and politicians were coming and going. I heard some MLAs were there. There was talk that Chief Minister Jyoti Basu had visited. Even the minister Rajesh Pilot had come. The Lal Bazaar police was all over the place. We stood outside Ganguram Sweets and watched from a distance. It was a horrific site of chaos.

We heard that the number of dead bodies was in the hundreds, but officials were citing fewer than fifty initially. There was a shanty behind Sardar ki baari where some three hundred people made khus-khus curtains for a living. They had all died. The people who died in the baari were being taken to the nearby Mughal Darbar hotel, where their bodies were being kept for identification.

Kamandal aapa's son Kallu was one of the deceased. I went with her to see his body. He was holding a packet of gutka in his hand. Bano aapa's damaad, son-in-law, was another body we saw.

He was Parveen's husband. I think his name was Maqsood. The air-conditioner had fallen on him and charred his face.

Later, we heard that Kallu had given two boys a package and asked them to store it in the underground basement where some bombs and ammunition were kept. He had told them to be careful with it. They were drunk and started fiddling with it. They dropped it. Boom! It exploded.

The bigger story that emerged later in the news was that Rashid was boiling with anger since the demolition of the Babri Masjid in 1992. He was in touch with Dawood Ibrahim in Pakistan. Kallu, Laala and Imtiaz had gone to the airport to receive a package from a stranger from across the border. It contained RDX. The Bombay bomb blast had taken place just a few days ago, on 12 March. Twelve explosions destroyed Bombay. A similar operation was being planned across major business districts in Calcutta. Bada Bazaar was the main target because it was a Hindu-dominated area. The carelessness of the two boys in the basement had saved the city from more damage. Laala and Imtiaz, Rashid's two main accomplices, fled to Bangladesh and never returned.

Rashid was arrested. He was convicted and sentenced to life imprisonment by the terrorist and disruptive activities (prevention) (TADA) court. But I think he keeps coming out on parole.[3] I have not met Bano aapa in a long time.

Many kothas in the area were affected because of the blast. The bais in Ramkali ki baari, Sattawandi, Chaudhari ki baari, Shambhunath ki baari all stopped their mujras. Many moved out, left the city. For a while, it seemed as if the kafan, shroud, had been spread not only on the dead, but also on the kothas of Bow Bazaar.

---

3   Katyayani, '1993 Bow Bazaar blast convict, terrorist Rashid Khan granted 90 days parole in WB', HinduPost, 25 April 2020, https://hindupost.in/news/1993-Bow   Bazaar-blast-convict-terrorist-rashid-khan-granted-90-days-parole-in-wb/

A funereal silence took over. I think it was the beginning of the end of the kothas.

Putput and his lousy fellows were still trying to clean the kotha in Bandook Gully. The blast had provided them with the ammunition to target us. We had to find other means of survival. Patrons were no longer thronging Bow Bazaar, fearing that they would be collared and harassed by the police. The bais were moving to Sonagachi. Most bednis migrated to Mira Road in Bombay to seek work in dance bars, as that was the new source of income.

My dhanda had also dried up. By this time, I had several surgical operations of my own – my body was its own landmine, where one explosion or the other was taking place periodically. In one operation, one of my ovaries was removed; in another my gall bladder was removed. Then even the other ovary was taken out. One operation had to be conducted because my intestines had bundled up. The doctor said I was dancing too hard. With so many complications inside my body, I knew that it was giving up and I had to find another way to survive.

Along with Kothariji, a patron, who, for a change, I kept in my flat as my live-in partner, I started a home business. It was his idea, actually, as he had left his own family and needed a place to live and work from. Along with the poor Muslim women who lived on the terrace of the new building, we set up a colour-making unit in my flat. By day, we would mix coloured powders in tubs and containers, weighing and sealing them in packets. In the evening, an agent would take them to the Bada Bazaar market and sell it to dealers. These colours were used in thread dyeing.

Kothariji was nice to me in the beginning. He had left his wife and children in Jodhpur, and was trying to live on his own in Calcutta. He used to come to the kotha, but had never spent time with me before you were born. He had also disappeared for a while when I was with Khan saab. Kothariji and I began seeing each other after the Khan saab chapter was closed.

Putput came to know that I had another house, where I was running a small business. It helped the poor women nearby and provided me with a steady income. I also worked there, arriving from the kotha in the morning and returning home by evening. I had a maid in Bandook Gully to cook and clean.

Sometimes, in the evening, I would dress up and entertain patrons who came to visit Bandook Gully. They were mostly the loyal patrons who came for a drink and a chat. Putput would just not allow the musicians entry. Though we had the baaja and the tabla at home, we did not have the musicians to play them.

At times, I would just tap on the ghungroo for music and sing a nazm to humour my guests who insisted. It was at an uneventful moment like this that I decided it had become impossible to perform any more. I did not miss it as it faded without a warning, a whistle, like the one in Congress House, which never failed to alert us of our impropriety. In Bandook Gully, the music slowed down to the faint tinkling of the bells in our anklets, making their way between the kitchen and the gaddi to serve snacks to the last of the patrons.

As we began to wear less chunky anklets, the bells were reduced to just one or two, strung on a simple chain. One day, that tinny sound of the bell also got lost in the sounds trickling in from outside. One day, the 9 a.m. siren in a mill close by alarmed us, bringing to the kotha the din of normal life. A commercial building rose up on one side of the kotha, blotting the morning sun out. And then another residential building from the other side towered above it. The kotha began looking like a dark, grey, dry well, sinking deeper into a cold, bottomless abyss.

Kothariji went to Jodhpur to meet his family. He never returned. The business that I had started with him lost its manager. He never settled my dues. I had not been smart. I had invested in him and the business, and the place was mine. I had put everything at stake because I trusted him. Initially, we worked well as a team, but his disappearance ended my dreams. Because I was not educated, he played me. I did not know how to run the business alone. I could not trust another man.

In the declining years of the kotha, the bais were leaving or switching to dance bars. Some bais had managed to quietly integrate into mainstream society without a fuss. They rolled up their past into a thick razaai, quilt, bundled it up in a peti and stored it in a deep, dark corner of their memories, which was then selectively forgotten. I wanted to do the same. With Kothariji, I could think of a grihasti, a parivar. Put all of my life behind me and think only about yours. But it was not to be. When Kothariji left, you were tall enough to venture out on your own. You did not have good grades and you hated going to college, so I sent you to Shanna's house in Pimpri for a break. I did that for you to understand life was not going to be as clean and rosy as your boarding school. You spent nearly two years growing up in that squalid Pimpri atmosphere, returning only for your college exams.

You helped me rent the flat out to your school friend from Darjeeling who was also studying here. You completed your college with a degree in Arts, which I always thought would be of no use to you. Do you remember that time I had telephoned you after I'd sent you to Pimpri to meet my sisters? Your college had sent me a letter saying you had won a graduation prize. I was so happy that I called Khan saab. He said he would like to speak to you too. On the call, you said you were surprised as well – what could the college be giving you a prize for? Not attending college, you laughed. You had never won a prize in school. It was an awkward conversation you had with Khan saab, who was on conference on the phone. Talk to papa, I surprised you. Whose papa? you asked. Yours, who else!

I shot back. Oh, you said, and asked him how his children were. Are you not his child? I asked you back. Your silence was not an affirmation. I could sense you had grown up. Khair, I attended the college function where they gave you a prize for scoring high marks in English. I felt so proud.

When I visited Pimpri, you had started working in Yerawada. You said it had something to do with writing about surgeries. I was happy that you were going in the right direction. I still remember the company's name – Deepak Nitrite! But you did not want to sign a contract with the company, so you quit without pay and insisted we return to Calcutta.

You came back and tried working as a salesman in a clothing store or two, but left them soon as well. You tried several jobs, including one of a car-wax-polish salesman, but you did not like it. I was worried about what you would do in life. But you got a job at the Oberoi Grand as an admin staff. You wore a tie to work and looked so smart. Everyone in the kotha was jealous of you, working so hard in a five-star hotel. Phullo gossiped that you were washing dishes, but that only made you laugh. You met filmmakers and artistes and politicians, and spoke to them in English. Phullo's sons had not made any use of their English-boarding-school education. You had. That made all the difference. You then got another job as a call-centre executive in Citibank. I was thrilled. I thought you were going to be a banker, if not a doctor; it was still a good job!

I continued renting out the flat to new tenants with the help of a broker after your friend left. The income it generated was sufficient for me to survive while living in Bandook Gully. What expenses did I have? Nothing! I lived very frugally. You were also doing well.

Dilip sir, a polite Bengali man, who was also, like Lal saab, once the branch manager of Allahabad Bank in Central Avenue, was one of my last and most loyal patrons. The old man, who was in his seventies by then, visited me quite often. He helped me understand and manage my finances. He never asked me for anything in return. He was the finest gentleman I knew. He died a few years later, after gifting me a diamond nose pin – like the one Khan saab had stolen from me.

I was the last courtesan to leave Bandook Gully. By the time I had to leave, everything was over. You had left long ago to work in a Gurgaon call centre, and then never returned to the city. The kotha was in a shambles. At last, Putput offered me fifty thousand rupees to vacate the room. His five children had grown up; his two brothers had two or three children each and they all wanted a floor each because of their own differences. The joint family needed more space, but within the same building.

In the time that you left, I found myself once again living alone on the first floor, with all other rooms shut. It was just like how it was in the beginning. I looked after a few stray cats that visited me regularly. They were the only friends I had left. I wore Dilip sir's gifted nose pin and looked into the mirror, counting the many creases and wrinkles that time had strewn on my face. The diamond glinted like a humbling, sacred truth.

Afterword

This memoir was recorded and written in 2020–21. My mother died on 14 February 2023. She suffered a cardiac arrest. She had various health complications and was on dialysis for some time. Her last words to me were, Montu, main marne waali hoon. Son, I am going to die. Even in her final moment she did not sugar-coat her truth and accepted it like a warrior. I missed my chance to say 'I love you, mummy', which I had probably never said to her in those exact words, but I do say it now, each passing day, aware that she has taught me to be more expressive. She chose a day of love, Valentine's Day, to leave. No one loved me like she did, and I fear I won't be able to love anyone as much as I understand and love her now. What a beautiful, brave and extraordinary woman!

Acknowledgements

Thanks to Kanishka Gupta, Arindam Ghatak, Bhaskar Chattopadhyay, Abhishek Majumdar and Shubham Roy Choudhury for being the first people to push the idea of the book. Arundhati Ghosh and Tanveer Ajsi at the India Foundation for the Arts, without whose gracious grant and incredible support this book would not have been written. Karanjeet Kaur for commissioning the essay for the website Arré that led to the book. Adrija Bose, Shweta Sengar, Mahtab Alam, Sanjay Dubey, Sreyashi Mazumdar, Arunima Maharshi, Bharat Nayak and Chinki Sinha at *Outlook*, who carried versions of the story in various publications.

Agent Anish Chandy, who should consider moonlighting as a motivational guru. Associate publisher–editor Swati Chopra at HarperCollins India for embracing this book wholeheartedly. Jyotsna Raman and Ujjaini Dasgupta for the wonderful edits, proofs and guidance in shaping the book.

To the incredible women who have stood with me: Sweta Pradhan, Mona Sherpa, Namrata Sundaresan, Shillpi A. Singh, Punam Sawhney, Tisha Chatterjee, Sharon Ishika Ghose, Shivani Tomar, Inayat Shaikh, Jyoti, Shama, Pasha Zamma and Rekha Bhardwaj. And to the few good men left: Priyanshu Jora, Assad Dadan, Kim Koshie, Anup Pandey, Mohit Dochania and Farhan Zamma.

Excerpt from the author's forthcoming title

My earliest memory of my father is also the most inextinguishable, like a wild forest fire.

A man got out of bed and stood in front of me. A woman sat behind me, adjusting her petticoat, and miraculously switched on the single yellow bulb hanging from the ceiling. I could tell it was my mother from the silvery sounds of her bangles and anklets – the music was home to my ears.

Turning around would have made me catch my mother in the act. I was too groggy to be surprised. Our living space was so tiny, and yet we had to often accommodate an unwelcome guest in bed, even when there was no room for more.

Where was my cot? I did not have one – or we could not afford one – but the easiest explanation would be that mothers like mine did not believe in sleeping away from their only child.

But who was this stranger before me – tall, bushy and naked?

He smiled. Kya dekh raha hai? What are you looking at? He asked.

He stooped to pick his trousers up from the floor and hunched over to wear them. A thick gold chain around his neck glinted in the dim light; his smile grew distinctly creepy as he fumbled with his pants.

Did I stare at his genitals when he questioned me? What was I looking at?

Here was a naked man who was having sex with my mother a while ago. I was lying next to them, turned away from the sight, but not the sounds. My ears soaked in the metal sounds jangling with huffs and moans to build a rhythm. The sounds of coruscating flesh flung meteoric sparks across my closed eyelids. Two bodies slamming into one another, trying to enter each other, but a door shutting in their faces every time they tried to pass through. And so they continued indefatigably, sweating and smelling of liquor and fading jasmines.

What I heard was painting pictures – there was a voyeuristic thrill in connecting the senses to a visual performance. Pupils adapt in the dark as they feel the sensations clouding their whites. The heightened senses of sound, touch, smell and taste are what make us inveterate nocturnal creatures, willing to substitute sight in return for its favours.

Who climaxed first?

A silence arose from their clammy loins. Heat escaped as vapour into the room. A stench reached my nose. It had the salty scent of something either sacred or sinful – I could not tell the difference. Thick clouds of frankincense hung in the air. Their heavy breaths were taking cognisance of what had transpired in the room. There was no snapping sound of a condom coming off.

The man walked out of the door. The light was switched off. I went back to sleep without a word exchanged between mother and me. There was no need to. I was certainly not going to remember the incident the next morning, or the one after that – it happened so often that one recollection was enough to cancel out all the other instances when my bedtime was interrupted by a post-coital kerfuffle.

I believe that is the first time I encountered a naked stranger in my bed. He had a boozy loftiness that comes from knowing too little in the exultant moment, but he did not register to me as a man out of his skin. He smelt like home.

My mother was his mistress. He came for sex. She gave him love. She gave him me, a drowsy child to a father who occasionally shared the only bed we had in the tenement, and who never kissed us goodnight before walking out of the door.

It has been more than thirty years since I last saw him. Except once, briefly, at sixteen, when I returned from the boarding school in Darjeeling, I insisted on meeting him. I went to his shop with a birthday cake.

It is my birthday, I said.

Here, he said, pulling out a fifty-rupee note from his wallet and giving it to me. I felt unwanted. I slapped the note on his desk and said, I had come to celebrate my birthday with you, not for your money.

And to think that this man once had the gall to suggest to my mother that she name me Aurangzeb. As if he was the Shah Jahan of paternal love!

I turned and left, not turning around to look. I have not turned around till date.

Many, many years later, when poet Nida Fazli died, and when I was working as a reporter, I was summoned to write a quick obit piece for Scroll.in.

Fazli's poem *Walid Ki Wafat Par* begins with the line, 'Tumhari qabr par main fatiha padhne nahi aaya' – I have not come to read a prayer on your grave. He wrote the poem for his deceased father, whose funeral he could not attend. It had inspired me to write a poem for my father whose funeral I will probably never be invited to attend.

It must be something to do with mourning those we do not see, but seek. Fazli's father migrated to Pakistan after Independence. They never met thereafter. My father abandoned me right after I was born. I am sure he is alive now, but I do not know if he exists. He ceased to long ago. Fazli wrote for his father, 'Tumhari qabr mein main dafan hoon; tum mujh mein zinda ho, kabhi fursat miley toh fatiha padhne chale aana.' I am buried in your grave; you live inside me, come and say a prayer for me if you find the time.

I suppose I am conveying a message to my estranged father through Fazli's death, who was once transmitting the message to me through his father's demise. About sons paying for the sins of the fathers.

Several years ago, when I was only beginning to imagine a life as a writer, it would have never occurred to me that one day I would be writing about Fazli. Alas! When he is dead.

But writing heals.

I am not even sure if new of my father's death will ever reach me. Earlier, I reacted to Nida Fazli's entombing poem and wrote, Zinda dil tab hoga, jab tum uth kar padh do gay fatiha jaage huay ek laash ke liye. Alive my heart will thence be, when you shall arise and recite a requiem for the living dead.

About the Author

Manish Gaekwad has worked as a journalist for such publications as Scroll.in and *Mid-Day*, and freelanced for *The Hindu*. This is his second book. His first novel, *Lean Days*, was also published by HarperCollins India in 2018. He has written a web series, *She*, with filmmaker Imtiaz Ali on Netflix, and is currently working as a senior script creative at Red Chillies Entertainment. He lives in Mumbai.

30 Years *of*

HarperCollins *Publishers* India

At HarperCollins, we believe in telling the best stories and finding the widest possible readership for our books in every format possible. We started publishing 30 years ago; a great deal has changed since then, but what has remained constant is the passion with which our authors write their books, the love with which readers receive them, and the sheer joy and excitement that we as publishers feel in being a part of the publishing process.

Over the years, we've had the pleasure of publishing some of the finest writing from the subcontinent and around the world, and some of the biggest bestsellers in India's publishing history. Our books and authors have won a phenomenal range of awards, and we ourselves have been named Publisher of the Year the greatest number of times. But nothing has meant more to us than the fact that millions of people have read the books we published, and somewhere, a book of ours might have made a difference.

As we step into our fourth decade, we go back to that one word – a word which has been a driving force for us all these years.

Read.

50 Years?

HarperCollins Publishers India

At HarperCollins, we believe in telling the best stories, and finding the widest possible readership for our books in every format possible. We seem to publish a great deal, but choose more than that: but what that's required, that is, the reason without which authors write their books in the first place, with which it derives reputation, and the respect, and the concern that we as publishers feel in being a part of the publishing process.

Over the years, we've had the pleasure of publishing some of the best-known writers in the subcontinent and around the world, and some of the finest thinkers in India; publishing is our own stories and authors have, with a phenomenal range of wonderful authors who also have been named Publisher of the Year, the greatest honour of time. But nothing else means more to us than the fact that millions of people have read the books we published and somewhere, a book of ours might have made a difference.

Hope you are our own, here too, we give our best to that; our work, the proof: what you see in your hands now is so; all the while...

HCI